AWAKENING TO LOVE

BOOK II

How to Trust in Love and Relinquish Fear to Help Humanity Live in Global Unity.

SIMON HERFET

Copyright © Simon Herfet 2019. All rights reserved.

No part of this book may be reproduced in any form or by any electronic or mechanical means, including information storage and retrieval systems, without written permission from the author, except for the use of brief quotations in a book review.

You can contact Simon Herfet at his website at:

https://simonherfetauthor.wordpress.com/

ISBN: 9781081176112

Table of Contents

FOREWORD 1

INTRODUCTION 4

THE SPIRITUAL COMMUNITY 10

THE DANCE OF UNITY 21

THE OCEAN OF BEING 42

LOVES LOST HOPE 50

PASSED THE EDGE OF DARKNESS 56

THE SPELL OF MATTER 60

THE COSMIC SHIFT 72

RETURN FROM THE VOID 83

THE DIVINE SOUL WITHIN 88

THE CHANGE IS HERE NOW 94

THE SPIRITUAL DIGITAL REVOLUTION 105

TRUST IN LOVE AND RELINQUISH FEAR 110

SHARING THE HUMAN EXPERIENCE 117

MOVING FORWARDS IN TIME 123

OUT OF DARKNESS INTO LIGHT 130

REPLENISHING THE SYSTEM 135

THE WOMB OF GOD 139

TRUST IN THE PROCESS 142

SURRENDER TO DIVINE POWER.......................... 149

THE GATEWAY OF DIVINE UNION 154

THE SYNCHRONICITY OF NOW.......................... 158

MOVING TOWARDS PLANETARY UNITY.......... 163

A GLIMPSE INTO THE FUTURE............................ 167

FOREWORD

This, my second book is a continuation of channelled messages by my 'higher-self' and in a similar fashion to the messages relayed in my first book of this series, called 'Awakening to Love,' which was published by Balboa Press UK.

I found the process of writing my first book challenging because throughout the process that writing a book entails, many fears, doubts and obstacles can arise, especially concerning one's own level of self-belief about bringing such a book into realisation.

Having succeeded in doing that, I have learnt that a book once produced and launched into the world, must prove itself on its own merits. However, in this case as the book primarily came through me, rather than from me, I have simply had to learn to let go and trust in the process and the forces of creation which led to its own fruition. As in 'Awakening to Love' – Book 1, the information for this follow up book in the Series came through me from the ocean of consciousness, which is what I believe we all share at the deepest level of our being and awareness.

This book had been 'gestating' in my mind for many years and I always knew what the essence of the message would be about. However, I did not know the format which it might take. Indeed - for many years in fact, I thought that it might take the form of a novel but a suitable story never came into my mind. A format of questions and answers turned out to be the result.

Initially, I had some misgivings about this method to relay the type of information that I wished to share for various reasons but in the end this type of format felt like a natural choice for me. The reasons for which, will be explained more fully later in the text.

Anyone briefly surveying the method through which this information is relayed to a part of my consciousness by some greater aspect of 'self', which is I believe shared by all beings, could perhaps still be excused for thinking that this method of access to the information is somewhat unusual or weird. However, as the writer, I trust wholly in the process and the essential truth of the nature and content of the information brought forth in this way.

At the end of the day, much of our great art, literature and music, is, I believe, 'channelled' by the individuals concerned from somewhere, sometimes from seemingly outside of their own self.

During my life, one of the most useful skills which I have acquired is meditation and it has helped me in so many ways. It is primarily I believe, the method which has helped me the most to develop the ability to bring through this information. Maybe though it is also a gift which I was born with. Irrespectively, my main wish is to use it to help others and so, in relaying this information to a world in which a multitude of people are suffering from a 'spiritual famine', I do hope at least, some of the information contained in this book will help to either dispel or diminish such hunger.

Simon Herfet

Regarding the content of this message, I ask the reader to listen to their own intuition as much as possible - as they read the information delivered here – as to whether the information is acceptable to themselves, and if not of course to simply move on to whatever resonates more with their own truth.

Finally, I should clarify the meaning of the initials 'S.H', for they represent the initials of the author (these denoting my questions) and those of 'H.S', represent the term 'Higher-Self' (denoting the answers given to me) which I whole heartedly believe to be the source of the replies to my questions. The essence of the meaning of the term 'Higher-Self,' being that part of my own greater soul which has a more direct connection to the soul of the world or 'all that is'. All that I will add at this juncture is to say that the awareness that is yours reading these words, is in fact the same shared awareness I believe, which at the deepest level channelled the replies to the questions revealed in this book. This is because, we all share the same ocean of consciousness which not only created us all, but also sustains 'ALL THAT IS'!

INTRODUCTION

We live in a time of great change. However, you could easily argue that all times are such. We move hopefully, from one present moment to another with grace, flow and elegance, in an ideal world. However, few of us see the world in this way. We look around us, and if we use the media as our sounding board, or our window onto the world at 'large', what we see is more likely akin to a world of chaos and discord all around us all. This however, is viewing the world as we see it through the myopic lens of the belief system and the profit machine with the intent of serving our soul's, a plate of 'daily fear' to produce our daily serving of anxiety. This in turn simply crushes each day our own core of self-potential if we let it and instead of seeing it self-realised, it is returned to its unopened box. We are simply left with the hope and belief that maybe tomorrow, one which never arrives, will serve us that helping of joy, peace, radiance and fulfilment which comes only from singing our own souls song, of actualization of our own full inner potential.

However, to make such manifest, in truth we must all learn to work hard and dig deep into our hearts and our souls to find our own inner-lions courage to face that which each of us in turn needs to face and pass through to help make our dreams come true and to be self-realised.

When we do that for ourselves, when we bring our dreams into reality, do we truly sense, really, truly sense, what we are capable of and how far each of us has travelled since our first step on this journey called 'life'?

**

S.H. "I would like to start by thanking you - my inner guidance, guide, spirit friend, higher-self, atma, Christ- consciousness, God even – call it what you will, for helping me with my book writing journey. I was told several times to 'trust in the process'. This I would like to think, I have done and I am continuing to do, as best I can. Though at times, challenging to do, it has been good advice. I thank you from my heart in so helping me with writing this series of books – be it that they are all yet to be completed – except for the first book titled 'Awakening to Love'."

H.S. "My son welcome back to the process, this process at large. We define it as such – because it has grown. Has it not my son?

You are also on a journey like all the rest, of your own self-discovery. Are you not, my son?"

S.H. "Yes, I am indeed".

H.S. You have had to learn new skills. You have had to face new challenges throughout the course of producing your first book. You have discovered that your dreams could come true. Have you not my son?"

S.H. "Yes, I have. I thank you from the bottom of my heart for helping me to write my first book, to help enlighten others to 'who they really are' – an eternal spiritual essence of being, shared by all."

H.S. "Indeed my son. That is who you are and in fact who you all are and share. For make no mistake the essence of which you speak, is shared. And it is shared by all of creation. Creation does not stand still. It is constantly creating, growing, changing, evolving. For this is the process and the pattern of life. It has always been so and it will continue to always be so. Things do not stand still, because the purpose of awakening to the spirit within is the engine which drives change. Although it is not obvious to you or most people, it is the reason for so much of what you see around you – whether it be news stories in your media, or quite simply what happens in your own backyard, so to speak. Life is a journey through change. Change is a pattern and the constant pattern of life. Without change, there is no growth. That is why change exists. That is the purpose of change. There is no other purpose for change, except to drive growth, forward. For make no mistake – growth does drive change and change in turn always leads to growth – although this may not always be the most visible or obvious outcome of such.

The purpose of this book, like your previous book is to drive growth and change in a forward direction. Never backwards. your society is still on the cusp of a great change. A revolution in consciousness raising in fact over recent years and for all human society. The young are now the drivers of this shift in consciousness as they are the prime surfers of this swift wave which now washes over your lands. In its attempt to clear that which is old, is of no use any longer. It belongs in the past. Old thoughts, old outworn ideas of old have had their time. Have had their day. They are no longer required. They have served their purpose. All those who gave birth to such ideas, have also too.

So, my son, you live in the dawning of a new age, of a new consciousness being born now. See it through and help with its initial development here as we explain to you in this and other books to follow this one – what we wish to explain to you here, is how and why such changes will and should unfold, for the betterment of society and that of the world at large."

S.H. "I am not sure what you are referring to here exactly. I have got a little lost here I think?"

H.S. "Well, my son. Your purpose with this as with the previous book is to help to 'awaken' others to who they really are. Correct?"

S.H. "Yes, it is".

H.S. "We are moving forward then beyond that process. We are taking you to the next stage of how and why society should move and change because of this greater spiritual awakening, to help to improve your human society and how it lives and treats your environment on planet Earth."

S.H. "Which is?"

H.S. "A new way of living based on a new way of thinking."

S.H. "Which is?"

H.S. "A way of inclusivity, rather than exclusivity. A way of sharing rather than a way of hoarding. A way of seeing, rather than a way of being led blindly through life and all that life throws at you, or your societies."

S.H. "Such as?"

H.S. "My son, for eons of time, humanity has thought primarily of 'self': selfish thinking rather than community thinking. This is the shift, the change which primarily needs to be enacted now. It is the shift back to community living. On whatever level, possible. From the smallest to the largest. For in essence, all the people of planet Earth. All human beings, in fact all creatures on your planet belong to one community. Whether you or they live on land or in the sea – you are all 'ONE COMMUNITY', at the deepest level. The spiritual - consciousness level. As you all begin to awaken – and one of the symptoms if you like, is that the awakening occurring within the self, is the greater awareness of 'community'.

As each person in turn sees themselves as part of such, a healing occurs. A healing within self and the greater self of which all are part. Your community, no matter how small or large is by definition of the larger community, the one community of souls which is ultimately the community that you might call 'God'. God's community is the ocean of souls being harvested for the riches they hold and in turn are being encouraged to share, to help the rest of creation for its own upliftment towards ever further and further self-realisation of the love you all share with the creator."

THE SPIRITUAL COMMUNITY

S.H. "My first book was titled "Awakening to Love" and was published on the 20th November 2018. Prior to the end of that year, there appeared to me at the time I thought, quite a lot of attention placed on my book. Between Christmas and New year of 2018 it reached 12,949th on the Amazon sales rank out of over six million books. I was excited and pleased at the time.

Between these dates, I felt strong waves of excitement due to the idea that my book was reaching so many people. Even if that was just people viewing some of its details online and especially as it was the first book that I had published. At the time, I was unaware exactly of how well or not my book was selling to the public at large. In retrospect, I wonder if the excitement I was feeling on many of those days was in fact the energy of connection with possibly many people who either purchased my book, as I thought erroneously that they had at the time, or were simply viewing it online. Is that possible? Is that what I was feeling then?"

H.S." My son, what you were feeling then was in fact a divine connection with the group consciousness involved in that and in fact this time too, whereby people as you suggest globally were viewing, reading or interacting with your books general material in some way. The loving vibration of themselves you were picking up on a subconscious level. There is an attunement to yourself, by those others interacting with your material on a spiritual energetic level. It all comes down to love at the end of the day. You are sharing their love generated by the essence of the material that you have helped to manifest in this material realm through the new-found existence of your book."

S.H. "Thank you. I did feel that I was picking up on an unusual feeling or energy, that I had not experienced before. I tried to suppress the feeling at first, as it almost felt too much for me to cope with. It was a bit overwhelming. I had to go into over-drive with my meditations to keep on an even keel. After a short time, I just tried to think of it as a wave on the ocean and that I should just try to be like a surfer and surf each wave of excitement as it arose and let go and enjoy the feeling. I knew it would not last forever."

H.S. "Yes, indeed my son. That was, and is the best approach to take at such times. Go with the flow. Don't try to stop the flow!"

S.H. "So, back to community then. We were talking about the largest community on this planet. The human or global community of being".

H.S. "Yes, my son. We were indeed. The topic you have just mentioned above connects us with this theme too.

All are connected through love. The love you share comes and goes in an external loop. Love can never run out. It is an energy and force of knowingness and divine benevolence. It is the gift which keeps on giving to you all. It is that which you all crave, yet at the same time can hold for free within your own hands for 'SELF' whenever you choose to do so. Open your hearts – open your minds – it is of your choosing whether you do so in any given moment. Love is always available to you all in each moment of your choosing. You are all made of love. It is love which is the force which holds each cell of your bodies together, so that they function in an orderly and healthy way. It is the intelligence inherent in each cell of your being which allows you all to be alive now. Your bodies are the gift that the creator has given to you all, to express joy and for you to experience such in this lifetime that you find yourselves in now.

Your community of being i.e. the human family, is the total expression of this human manifestation. It is each individual's choice whether they see themselves as part of a unified peaceful family of humanity, together or not. In the same way, you choose in your blood family whether to create peace or hostility. So, it is with the larger human family. Do you focus on what connects you all or what you erroneously perceive to focus on - that which you imagine to disconnect you all?

We use the word 'erroneously,' for that is what such focus is. For what you perceive to be the disconnect is not in fact true, irrespective of race, colour, class or creed. You are all one human family in the eyes of God.

So, my friends see yourselves now, with these eye's. The eyes you do truly behold. The only eye's which you truly had or have now in this life. For in truth only one being looks out through all eye's. The same one being you all share, and are, at the deepest level of your being possible to experience. For you are, each of you, embodiment of that, in human form. You are atma, you are soul, you are spirit, you are consciousness projected from a human form, gifted and made manifest through you all – so that God can experience through you all, in this physical universe of magnificent manifestation of physicality, in which you now dwell. You are God's community of 'ONENESS'.

S.H. "Beautiful words, those. But how can we get those people, still to awaken, to this deeper level of reflection and projection?"

H.S. "My son it starts with belief. It starts with self-belief in fact. Belief in the true self. The divine self."

S.H. "Yes, in the country and society in which I live, the U.K.- this type of thinking is really very rare, I am sad to say. We need a sea change really. A massive shift in our thought and consciousness, for people to have this sort of self-realisation".

H.S. "Yes, my son you do. But you are helping to bring about this sea change along with many others, with your book here, are you not?"

S.H. "Yes, I hope so. But they still only reach a limited number of people. Plus, I never know to what effect. How many people can and does my book help towards this new paradigm – this new consciousness- this new, more peaceful Earth?"

H.S. "Many my son, much more effect than you realise. The shift taking place is coming from so many directions, through so many people now. You are partaking and playing your role in this 'sea-change', as are many others. In many varying, myriad ways of being, behaviour and types of creativity. Whether it be through music, art, literature. Kind actions by one person for another in every way imaginable."

S.H. "How could we change the structure or the methodology of how we run our communities, either at the smallest or the largest level to best facilitate change in this sort of way?"

H.S. "A change of consciousness in the governments of your choosing, is key in this change. The consciousness of the people, reflects the consciousness of the leaders. As the consciousness of your societies grow so will it be reflected in the type of consciousness of the leaders you choose at any given time. It will be through them and the teams of people whom they choose to support them, that change will come.

Education needs to change too, to help support the growth and change of consciousness which is coming and needs be sustained. You cannot expect to teach your children the same as they were taught centuries ago and expect them to leave school and university with a different consciousness to the generations which preceded them. So, the curriculum taught needs to reflect the change desired.

If you wish for greater wisdom, harmony and peace in your communities in your families, in your countries, in your world - then the young must be educated that 'all are one'. THAT ALL CREATION IS CONNECTED."

S.H. "Surely then this means teaching an inclusive, almost new religion. A new type of religion. One not encased by 'dogma' or 'creed', surely?"

H.S. "Yes, my son, as you are doing so elegantly here now – upon and within these very pages. But these words are not limited to here. To this book. To these pages alone. For these words and similar are blowing on your winds, through the trees and minds on many lands right now. They are settling like a new 'dew' of a new consciousness into the minds of many. Stirring an awakening, to a remembering of something forgotten. Not of something unknown to them. For humanity, as always, is just being helped to remember who they are. Divine manifestations in human form of the mother-father creator – God!"

S.H. "So please continue. Explain further how this raising of human consciousness of our spiritual connection and awareness of such can encourage more of the same."

H.S. "My son, it is already growing like seeds in the minds of men, women and children across your lands. Like a new fertile crop of a new expectation, of a new Earth, and a new beginning. Sometimes a new beginning goes unnoticed by many. Yet even if so unnoticed, it is real. Look out - look out far beyond the limitations of your own mental horizons of understanding. Acknowledge the change in attitudes, especially in the younger generations to your own about so many facets of your life. Changes across your globe about health and wellbeing. This including knowledge spreading like a cancer of 'wisdom', instead of a cancer of 'death'. The knowledge and awareness of too much stress in society being a fundamental weakness to the structure of the individual's mind set of wellbeing. Wellbeing is dependent on a bed-rock of 'peace' under-pinning your everyday lives. Otherwise you <u>cannot</u> live in a healthy society. Peace must begin in the individual and so it is spread across your societies base. Society's base begins at home with the family. It spreads to your communities of town and cities. From your countries to continents and ultimately your globe. Your planet. Your only home of choice. For choose, you most surely must. For in the dim distant recess of memory within the very structure of your planet, there the knowingness of memory within it, recalls a time long lost to humanity's memory of how nature – your natural world once existed. Before humanity, through its arrogance and self-pride believed it could simply 'take', without consideration of giving back.

Now though the wheel of destiny has turned full circle and you find yourselves back where you started in some respects. By this we mean, that as humanity awakens further to its new-found potential, through mass spiritual realisation of your true nature, eyes, minds, and ears are once again opened to things that so many refused to see or acknowledge to needing, to see changes made not only in your very bodies. For as you have thrown rubbish onto your lands will exist for lifetimes, such as the many varieties of plastic waste, but also the pollutants you use on your crops, which you then consume, and in turn leads to a host of diseases, for many of these chemicals are killers. They are used to kill insects and microbes not wanted, to help your crops last longer. If these chemicals kill such things, then why imagine that they will not also kill humans in time?

However, this shift to greater awareness affects not just the body but mind also. For as your bodies work more, as they were always intended to - as the beautiful creations as the creator intended for them to operate at their highest level of intention and grace, so humanity's connection with the spiritual essence within you all also will be clearer and more able to guide you as was always intended."

S.H." Also, now so many are being drawn by their electronic and digital devices away I feel from being 'present'. What do you have to say about this and its likely effect on the lives of younger people so addicted to them now?"

H.S "My son, these devices you are correct- are a distraction to that which is going on around you all at any one time. It takes your attention to that which you choose to place it on shown on the device in question. You are drawn often through boredom and the desire to escape that which you so often perceive to be your 'hum-drum' lives.

Instead of seeing your lives as such – instead endeavour to change your lives, instead of reading about the lives or circumstances of others, either for the better or worse. For each moment wasted is a lost opportunity of mindfulness in action, rather than inaction. For the time spent on devices is in the main, is time spent 'inactive,' unless the purpose of the use of your time on such devices is to secure a better life and world for either yourselves, or others.

These devices in themselves are not a bad thing. It is how you use them and when you use them, about which you all need to be most aware.

Choose such devices when human company is not available but do not put such devices above others. They will always be available, but people will not be."

S.H. "How can we make community living more holistic, more organic. More spiritual than it currently is then?"

H.S. "My son, through self-awareness primarily. Awareness of who you are. Awareness of who you all are. That you are 'spirit', in a material body. That you are not the body. Not the mind. You are all consciousness existing in an ocean of conscious spiritual awareness of being. You are love. Awaken to this – your true nature. Let it shine out of all 'your' eyes. Each and every one of you. For you are all so much more than you ever believed possible, than you once thought.

Do not limit yourself, to the erroneous belief of histories landscape of doubt and insignificance. You, none of you are ever insignificant to, or in the mind of God. You are all <u>known</u> and <u>loved</u>

and <u>cherished</u>. More than you will ever know. As is your mother. So is God – mother to all – sustaining you all in each moment, each heartbeat of your very being.

So, cast aside any remaining mental shackles of any belief that you are not loved at any time. For you always were and always will be for eternity. For you are that essence which loves <u>you!</u>"

It is from such a base of solidarity and self-confidence that you move forwards into your new world of manifestation of change which your planet so hungers and desires. Many are on this path now, including those with the eyes that read this book now- otherwise you would not have been drawn to such. You are the seeker within, searching for the answers which you always knew but simply had forgotten. So, arise now brothers and sisters in spirit and reclaim your place beside me. The energy of your being. The energy which keeps you alive day and night, until I call your soul back to me - back from where your very birth arose and will arise again and again, many fold, until you're learning is no longer required and your soul chooses instead, a new, a different form of expressing, which exist in my being. For humanity's expression, is but one expression, in, an ocean of expressions of choice.

As I awaken now in you and each 'you' that you see around you, change will be the inevitable result. How can it not be?

It is of my choosing, you see. For it is 'I', and only 'I,' which expresses through all. Only one 'I'. We are it. We are that.

Awakening to Love

We always were.

We always will be.

You see!"

THE DANCE OF UNITY

S.H. "I feel my position in this process, to be a 'questioner,' rather than that of an 'interviewer,' as that does not feel appropriate in this process. I am fine with that for this process, these 'books' coming through me, are just that, I feel the words flow through me rather than from me. The more I can step out of the way the better the quality of the information that comes through me. I 'surrender' to and trust in the process".

H.S. "Indeed my son. Well said. You are being 'used' as a conduit for spirit to speak, to tell the story of old.

The story of old is the story of humanity and the story of your being. For your being has always existed you see, in the non-time of the present moment. For in truth there is no such thing as time. Time is a construct which holds your physical reality in a semblance of order, serenity and therefore peace. The result of a physical reality being brought into being nictitated 'time' also to be born. For time is a measurement of creation against the transparency of non-time of being. Let me explain this;

In the physical realm, you need time to show and explain that you are real. To use your own experience of life: you have a physical body which ages and eventually dies. This is measured and witnessed by the passage of 'time'.

In the etheric body, as your soul resides without a body, in the spirit realm there is no time. There is being, there is existence of awareness, but there is no 'time'. Therefore, you do not witness your soul, or any other age. Not just because there is no physical body, but because there is no time.

In your physical awareness and expression of being your body ages and dies. This is not because of the passage of time. It is because of the expression of 'death'. By this we mean that your belief in the passage of time and your belief in the certainty of 'death,' presents itself according to your belief that death is real. Because you believe in death, so it comes to pass".

S.H. "So, if we don't believe in death, then we won't die? Is that what you are saying? Because no one will believe that is true."

H.S. "Exactly my son. You cite the expected and usual reply. In your answer, you see how deeply engrained the belief that you will all one day die is entrenched in your thinking."

S.H. "So, is it the belief, that we age, is also the reason that we do age? That we grow old and die?

H.S. "Yes, and no. Your body grows because the body separate to your own self-awareness, has its own self-awareness entrenched in the wisdom of every molecule of your being. Your bodies DNA follows its own instructions of its own intelligence to do, create, heal and change every aspect of your body throughout its lifetime. You do not control this. Your body does without you 'stepping in', so to speak. It is all done automatically below your conscious awareness. It is done despite yourself. Is it not my son?"

S.H. "Yes, it is. That is true!"

H.S. "In the same way the body ages and eventually dies. Correct?"

S.H. "Yes, true."

H.S. "But what humanity does not acknowledge, is the role that they play in this pattern. The mind is very powerful as you are learning. You create your own reality according to your beliefs. In the same way, therefore you can change your reality with your beliefs, when they change.

When the belief of an individual is held in such a way – that is with total knowing, trust and certainty in a desired outcome, that outcome can be self-realised.

So, to explain further, using death as an example, what we are saying here, is that your reality as we explain it here is dependant, not on what you have been told, but what you 'yourselves' believe. Change your own belief and change your own reality. That is the key. It will not change it for others. But it will change it for you!"

S.H. "I have read about some people who are rumoured to have lived for hundreds of years. Those that come to mind, are the mystic named Babajii from India. Also, Count Saint Germaine who is rumoured to have lived for several hundred years, around the time of the eighteenth century.

Exactly, my son. They both developed this ability with their own minds to achieve such an outcome. They also held the power of manifestation of various physical objects. The power of such people includes raising people from the dead. Such things have been made manifest by various persons in your history, who you and others can research.

Here we are speaking about a very high level of personal evolvement. However, the purpose here is to explain the power over the mind. Or the power of the mind over your perceived physical reality."

S.H. "Yes, but surely this does not prove time is an illusion but that certain properties of time i.e. that time leads to death – can be overcome with the power of the mind, if developed sufficiently?"

H.S. "Yes, my son true. But what we are saying here is that time does not, 'not' exist but that it can be overcome, through a change of belief, or how you view the perception of such a thing as time. That time is not quite as you believe it to be."

S.H. "Ah, I see. So, time is real. But that time is not quite what we believe it to be?"

H.S. "Exactly. Time is a construct to make your world run smoothly and in an orderly way. It is the way life is organised by the creator. In the non-physical etheric world time is not required."

S.H. "Why not?"

H.S. "Because there is no need for time."

S.H. "Why not?"

H.S. Because the etheric world is not physically manifest. Is not physical, it exists in a different dimension to your own. Where the law of physics and being do not apply as in your own physical world. You cannot truly compare. The world of the etheric is, as is your world created in your dreams. It is created by your awareness on a different level of your being created by consciousness and not physically constructed. It is a totally different vibration on being, as is a dream to being awake. Yet, you know now from the clarity of your own dream recall, it can feel as real as your physical world. Yet, you know how different it feels to you. Also, within your dreams you do not sense any passage of time. Do you understand this my son?"

S.H. "Yes, I do. I can make a comparison of the two, now that I often recall some of my dreams. Whereas, once I hardly ever did. Then when I did it was only bits of my dreams. The experience of either or are very different, I agree. However, they are both different expressions of being or experience."

H.S. "Yes, my son. Again, we are limited here by the availability of words which you can use to explain this paradox of being. Which is, how do you explain an experience of being in a place of non, or no-time, who's only recalled experience is in a place where the passage of time exists? This is a very difficult thing to explain or express to another. It is like trying to explain the content of a television channel totally unlike the ones that you are familiar with watching. Is it not my son?"

S.H. "Yes, I see, I understand now. I wondered how on earth you were going to explain my question which led in to the description of this. It was a testament of my own trust and ability to see where the question led to in terms of the quality of the explanation given. I am happy with the answer given here. I do doubt at times how distinct from my own knowing these answers are. Simply put that they come from a higher source. Not my own mind. As much as I do not wish to dwell in a space of delusion. Neither equally important, do I wish the readers of this information to do so."

H.S. "Indeed my son, we bring you truth on the vibration of love which you send out each day my son."

S.H." Earlier today I was listening to a very interesting podcast by an American called 'Rich Roll'. He was talking to a scientist and doctor about degradation of the soil in many places and the overuse of chemical pesticides causing damage to enormous swathes of land, particularly in the United States, leading to the loss of much of their top soil. This in turn, impairing the growth and quality of crops where growing them is becoming more problematic. The man spoke of the many causes and issues surrounding this problem and how to overcome it. I can see that an obvious answer to this issue is stepping up education of the population about these issues and the human health problems that can result from the over use of pesticides. How can this and similar issues best be addressed by humanity at large please?"

H.S. "My son this is an important and very topical question right now. This same question already applies equally to your environments at large from a variety of sources of pollution. However, the source of the pollution is from humanity's actions and uses of such and similar materials including plastics too, of course.

There needs to be a sea change in humanity's use of such materials. This fundamentally is a question of teaching to raise the knowledge level of such practices and the harm that they do to your environment. As well as a host of wildlife and fauna, humanity will reap the cost to the detriment of their own health, until the issues causing them are sufficiently addressed. This cannot be done overnight. It involves consumers changing their spending habits by investing in more organically produced products across the board. Minimizing the use of plastics for packaging, recycling more whenever possible.

Teaching these issues needs to become a fundamental part of children's education. This is probably the most fundamental change, how society thinks and acts around these issues. This means lobbying your politicians and voting accordingly. It means the same on a global level. Education, education, education! That is the key. There is no magic fix. Except the removal of humanity itself!"

S.H. "Thank you. In other words, apart from the extinction of humanity, we must educate society to change the use of these chemicals to limit and ultimately stop this destruction to the environment and ourselves. It is human beings who have introduced them into farming practice in the first place. There has been a large global movement towards organic farming in many places around the world.

However, in places such as the United States of America, the grip of the big manufacturers and business corporations hold a lot of sway and power in keeping things as they are, especially to the people directly involved in the production of said crops who are getting more and more ill. I had not heard how bad things are getting in the U.S.A. until today's podcast. I strongly recommend people searching out the 'Rich Roll podcast' online, for a listen to educate themselves further about these types of very important issues."

H.S. "My son indeed. It is only through education about what needs to change that change will come!"

S.H. "I suppose this topic is still relevant to this chapter. For a coherent, healthy society or community, we must all pull together and educate each other as to what is or will be detrimental to our own survival. This obviously includes limiting that which is damaging to our communities of being. These chemicals are poison and we should choose other more organic methods for our food production and for the welfare of our future generations, the environment and the planet at large."

H.S. "My son everything is connected. A healthy society, breeds a healthy environment. A healthy environment breeds a healthy Earth – which in turn breeds a healthy human being. It is the circle of connection of which you all depend.

You are connected by the awareness – the consciousness which you all share. You cannot escape from this. You are one entity of being, be it expressing from an individual point of focus. This is the purpose of this book and others similar, is to regain your singularity of focus on the one consciousness which you all are, which you all share. On your only planet of choice."

S.H. "Is it really the only planet of choice then?"

H.S. "My son it is the only planet of choice in as much as you are all free to choose in each moment how you express your beingness. Whether or not you choose to do this, is another choice again. The reason we say this is because other more evolved societies choose from a higher group soul perspective. They make choices dependant on the overall good and wellbeing of their societies. You - humanity - in your world, make choices in the majority, based on the individual. Not based on the good of the community at large. Your society has not yet evolved to this higher level of choosing. Of placing the greater 'community' as your focal point. As your priority.

Hence the problems and issues arising as mentioned in your previous question about agro-chemicals and their harmful nature of use.

When such issues are dealt with by the group mind and consciousness, they are not chosen for obvious reason. Greed being the reason of choice when left to the individual alone.

My son, this is why you are the only planet of choice. 'Others', have chosen differently to move as one in their decisions, hence their greater evolvement. Your planet on which humanity is still evolving and is evolving towards this higher group consciousness. In time, you will see the wisdom of decision on a mass level towards its benefit towards your society. Then your choices are made through a group decision when major issues need to be decided. This in turn leads to even smaller individual decisions which always need to be made of course coming from a higher perspective of self-awareness."

S.H. "Over the course of this last weekend I have been listening to several very interesting podcasts that my wife has introduced me to, covering a lot of very important issues. One of them as previously mentioned was about the depletion of top-soil in many parts of the world, caused by the overuse of herbicides and pesticides, including the damage they cause to the health of humans and other creatures.

But, I am especially concerned about the effect on the global bee population world-wide. This needs to be addressed urgently!"

H.S. "You are right my son. Bees exist not for the benefit of humanity however. They exist because, in their own right, as an expression of the creator. Their pollination, is God's pollinating of many life forms, to be an expression of the creator to share with the world. They are all expressions of both beauty and wisdom. They are expressions of wisdom, because it is the bee's own intelligence which helps manifest and produce in turn, a further production of much of the flora and fauna around yourselves. In your world, in your countryside, in your woodlands even in your cities.

However, I repeat bee's and other similar insects were not placed on your Earth for your or human benefit. They are their own expression with their own purpose of self-replenishment. Their food source is the honey they manufacture and share as a gift to humanity. Humanity is free to share such within moderation.

However, the chemical usage of which you spoke earlier here is now harmful not just to the bee population, but to your species also, plus many others, due to these chemicals harmful effects on your eco-system. These chemicals are indeed being most damaging. There needs to be a severe limitation placed on their use, to either eradicate or greatly diminish this harmful effect on nature. These chemicals are like weapons of war-fare used on 'self'.

They are however, yet again a reflection of the consciousness of those who sanction their use for such purposes. Greed is an element for such use. However, farmers who spray and use them on their crops are in many cases hostage to financial debt and in most or many cases are to their own financial self-interest. The industries who produce the chemicals also make them for their own financial profit and do all in their power to continue their use, including their influence on politicians and such to ensure such continued use.

There is however only one answer to changing this situation. This is further education and presentation of the harm they are causing to <u>all</u> of you and to much of your creation and the creatures who come into contact with the said chemicals.

There are many other chemicals and materials that are being leached into your environment – be it land, water or bodily forms which is detrimental to the wellbeing of all, for similar reasons to the aforementioned ones. These all need to be addressed over time – the sooner the better. If you or anyone feels such is calling them, offer help wherever and however you can. For a call to action comes in many guises – each to their own my son!"

S H. "The problem with such issues I feel, is like so many pressing issues which need addressing by all countries. It once again seems to stem from a sense of apathy and sense felt by so many that they are all powerless to do much to address these bigger issues. As if these matters are so big that they are out of their hands. Things that only politicians can change?"

H.S. "My son, your own sense of powerlessness once felt, now feels like a sense of empowerment – does it not?"

S.H. "Yes, it does. This is because I have found my voice through writing a book and having it published for people to read. In so doing, I feel that I have found my own ability to express my voice through such, to hopefully inform a few people at least of a way towards positive change. That is my hope at least."

H.S. "Indeed it is my son. You have to learn to grapple with and defeat your own inner issues and blockages which formerly held you back from doing such. Correct?"

S.H. "Yes, correct. I had to fight through my own limitations of my own self-belief so that I in turn developed my own abilities to help bring change about."

H.S. "Indeed, my son and that is what others must endeavour to do also. When they manage such, they too can be an agent for change in their own area of choice, to help implement such change where they believe it is required. Each individual has their own calling, their own gift to share with the world. Their gift may not be to help bring change about. But say, rather to bring 'joy' to others. Yet in so doing they will uplift the 'spirits' of such people. This in turn can help nourish others in ways to help sustain them with their own projects at hand. In the same way bee's produce honey for self-nourishment, some of their honey is used by humans for self-nourishment."

S.H. "Is this not wrong though? Is it not taking away the bee's own food?"

H.S. "It is wrong, if it is detrimental to the bees themselves. If not, it is permissible. Follow your hearts on such issues, if it does not feel right to you, follow that prompting."

S.H. "Another of the issues I hear spoken about a lot, is the paradox about the use of our technological devices such as smart phones and lap-tops. So many people are spending so much of their time using them. We can all learn so much from them, but at the same time if they are not used in moderation, there must be a host of negative effects that they will have on us and on our relations with others if not used wisely?"

H.S. "Yes, the important word here is 'wisely'. They are useful in moderation and in relation to the purpose of usage. You cannot put the 'genie' back in the box so to speak. These devices are a distraction to the power of the present moment and all that that entails and offers, as covered in the first book of this series. The present moment is your true point of connection with the divinity within you all. Distraction is a good thing if it is healthy and useful, but not if done to excess – like any other activity. Moderation in all things my son."

S.H. "There seems to me, right now, a big shift going on. Yet another leap in the number of people waking up to their true spiritual essence of who they really are, as outlined here. Not just in this series of books – but many other similar ones too. I am filled with joy myself to have finally reached a point within myself to play an active part in this 'revolution' of higher consciousness. By that, I mean the way of the 'peaceful warrior' within, rising up to meet life's many challenges and problems which so many of us must face in our lifetimes."

H.S. "My son, welcome back to this 'dialogue on awakening' after your recent holiday. It is in fact over a year ago that you finished your book, which shall we say, 'we wrote together'. Yes, it is correct that 'you' are used as a channel for the answers to the questions that you set 'us' here. The answers are given to you out of your own love for the creator and because you have been asking, in your own meditations for many years now, to be used as a channel to help raise the consciousness of humanity. Is that not correct my son?"

S.H. "Yes, that is correct."

H.S. "You have also asked to be used as a teacher as well as a writer, and recently also as a speaker, to add to your opportunities in assisting spirit to attend to the task in hand, correct?"

S.H. "Yes, correct also."

H.S. "My son, we are assisting you in your efforts to do this to help you achieve your goals towards helping as regards this, as are many other individuals in many other ways also, in a similar fashion. So, we simply say to you, keep on keeping on with your efforts. A little bit each day, will in due course result in your second book being made manifest to continue to help others along their own spiritual path and help them with their own reawakening to who they truly are, but had merely forgotten for the briefest period of time.

All of humanity is now on the cusp of a still more greater awakening towards such, of an ever and ever greater degree. Your own refinement of your own spirit gift being used here to manifest your words to help others is indicative, not just of your own travails, but of that of others also. For all the hard work towards personal development of you all, is shared by you all at the deepest level of the collective of human consciousness. It is shared by you all, for the benefit of you all, you see. Nothing is wasted for good or bad. All actions have a consequence, whether for good or bad. As humanity now wakes up and rises to a new level of 'global being', a unity of greater peace and harmony will also prevail across your lands, with the result that more and more people will reach that point of consciousness, so to facilitate a mass awakening of souls to their true nature, than ever has occurred within the history of your world, my son. Though this may not be apparent to many of you in this moment of time, with much negative news coverage in your media. But do not forget all that is positive which is occurring right now. If your focus is more on this – that which is positive and points towards the current levels of awakening already prevalent in your world as we speak, such a revolution is already in place my son."

S.H. "Thank you, for these very timely and positive words. They fill me with great encouragement and of course help to encourage and motivate my actions still further to assist in this 'revolution of higher consciousness' of which you speak.

Can you give me advice how I can bring awareness of the availability of these books to the attention of more people to raise their own spiritual awareness?"

H.S. "My son, continue as you are. You are indeed doing a good job already. Allow 'spirit' to continue to guide your hand as you are doing right now with all your literary efforts. Ask beforehand and continue to ask for your own spiritual assistance with regards to such.

You can never know or see for yourself the true extent to which the forces of spirit are helping and guiding all those other beings out there towards your work and your efforts. They will be drawn to the resonance of your work. For those whom it resonates, likewise to their own vibration of being, so they will be drawn to your words. It is no use your work being in the hands for whom your words do not resonate, for they would be wasted. Trust as always in the process my son. This will take a little longer yet. However, success awaits you in your travails and you will not be disappointed with the outcome. We can assure you of that my son."

S.H. "Thank you again for your kind words of support. I know in truth that I only write the questions and the answers are given to me from spirit. The words just flow through me as a conduit. As my hand now flows so swiftly across the pages to keep up with this flow of information. For the information – the answers they just flow through me, usually entirely without pause, until whatever answer is finished. Then I am on to the next question of my choosing hopefully relative to the topic at hand and off goes the flow into the next answer here. That dear reader, is how this process is made manifest. I have asked to be used in this way for a long time – 'to help raise the consciousness of humanity'. That is what I believe can happen. Even if it is one person only who is helped by these words. Then that is a positive result."

H.S. "Indeed my son, your prayers have indeed been answered, as we provide the answers to your questions here. Not only here, but as guidance in your everyday life in the same way as all other people are guided by the divine light, love and guidance within themselves which is no different to your own guidance my son.

All are cared for, are nurtured by the great spirit."

S.H. "My wife and are I are now both getting more and more involved with our own writing careers. However, each of us struggle at times to balance our work and family time. I know many people struggle with organizing this. Can you advise here too please?"

H.S. "My son the best way is to set out in advance the purpose of your objectives in relation to such. For example, if financial advancement is your goal, then you should weigh the merits of such against the outcome. How much for example a greater satisfaction about your lifestyle will bring you?

However, if helping others is your main objective, then you will know that the purpose is to help others rather than to help your own self. In this course of effort, you must keep that balance of what is good for your own health and that of your family. You must prioritise your own and your family's well-being first, to ensure your platform of being is conducive to producing the work that you wish to manifest for the world. Otherwise this will become much more difficult to achieve, if not impossible for you to achieve."

S.H. "Yes, balance is the key. Finding the right balance between the two aspects of our lives."

H.S. 'Yes, indeed my son."

S.H. "How in my writing process, style of writing and in the questions I ask here, can I be most successful in helping to raise the consciousness of humanity towards more love and compassion?"

H.S. "Good question my son. Firstly, as we have previously said – you are endeavouring to help others to awaken to their true nature are you not?

This being that they are embodiments of eternal spiritual knowing consciousness and awareness, connected always to all that is – now – and throughout all time. Eternal aspects of the one God which is in essence who and what all of creation is now, always has been, and always will be. That is who you all are in truth. That said, so many still need to awaken to this fact in 'truth'. By that we mean the fact which 'truth' is. For what is 'truth'? What is the true definition of truth my son?

The true definition of truth is this: it is that which cannot be argued to be a lie.

By this we mean truth, is that which is irrefutable – that which cannot be denied or ignored. The truth can never be ignored, for that which is real, cannot be denied in truth. For no matter the degree of denial, the truth cannot, 'not be'. Because truth is truth. Truth is not a belief – it is that which is. A belief is that which might be, or could be, in the minds of those who hold said belief. A belief can also be truth. However, that which is truth, is always truth, by its own reality of being such. Therefore, truth will always be available to the 'seeker'. Because it is truth, it will always be available. A lie is never available in truth, because a lie does not exist in 'truth', for at the deepest level only 'truth' is real.

Therefore, to go back to your question. "What is the best way to way to help raise the global consciousness of humanity towards more love and compassion. First, people must discover the truth of their own nature and essence. Then all that springs from that, springs from truth. Therefore, more love and compassion will inevitably follow, for the gateway to truth has been opened within themselves to allow such to occur. This is because when you remember the truth of who you are, the barriers that were formerly there in your hearts towards others will be dissolved and love and compassion will flow more freely to others.

So, we here are endeavouring in the first instance to find 'their truth'. By this we mean, 'their truth' is the truth of all. For truth is truth, in this context of truth, there is only one 'truth,' as previously described.

This truth does not diminish any religion that exists, for all are correct in the sense that all of humanity exists in love and God loves all humanity, all creation and all that is, for that is 'God' or whatever you wish to refer to as 'Great Spirit', which holds you all in its tight embrace of eternal love, light and life."

S.H. "So the key is to help humanity connect and believe in 'truth'. That truth being the one and only 'truth' – that we are all connected as one conscious loving compassionate energy of being. Eternal, all-knowing and present throughout everything."

H.S. "Yes my son that is what you all truly are!"

THE OCEAN OF BEING

S.H. "I often use the analogy of the ocean, when I speak to others about my own spiritual beliefs. I particularly don't adhere rigidly to one religion or another. However, I respect them all. I personally believe in what I like to describe as the 'golden thread of truth', which I see as linking and running through all the world's religions and great spiritual teachings.

Sometimes as well, I like to use the analogy of the fish in the ocean asking, "where is this ocean?" I think many human beings are a bit like that too, when it comes to understanding what 'God' or whatever you want to call it is. To myself, God is a bit like what the ocean is to the fish in the ocean and it being unable to see God, due to the fact it is immersed in the ocean of water. Just as we are also similarly immersed in the creation of being all around us.

So, here in this this process we are trying to help awaken others who have yet to awaken to a greater knowing to who they really are. Of course, once we start to awaken to this greater realisation of our true self, I do believe it is inherent upon us to practice greater and greater love and compassion towards others. Otherwise, there is little point in awakening because people will simply continue as they have to date."

H.S "Indeed, that is true. The point of 'awakening to love', is to practise a greater degree of love and compassion. That is the natural consequence of such as you will feel more drawn not just to others of all colours, race and creeds. You will also feel a greater connection and respect for your environment and mother Earth."

S.H. "Now in my own country, there is a political battle ensuing which has been going on for over two years called 'Brexit'. This is about whether the people want the United Kingdom to leave the European Union, of which we have been a part of for the last forty-two years and after a vote was held and a narrow majority voted to leave. The opinion is nearly evenly split between the population of the United Kingdom. I feel that this is a part of a greater movement towards nationalism by some people rather than greater global integration, which is what I would prefer to see occur. Please advise."

S.H. "My son, there is a rise towards nationalism in some areas, you are right. This is indeed for many reasons. What many people fail to see, realise and understand, is that humanity and all economies are connected by default. You all exist on one planet and the economy of each country is very dependent on each other's. You cannot exist or operate as an economy, in harmony with others, if you move towards greater independence. That is a sign of national pride and self- service only, rather than global service. You are one family, one race. You are not a family of nations. You are <u>one</u> nation. The global nation, the human family. Your countries need to move towards greater and greater harmony of integration not the polar opposite. Countries want independence often for purely economic self-interest. To deregulate their economies to compete more deeply with other economies. This self-serving practise is disadvantageous to the majority as a few reap a great financial reward. The profits are not spread evenly to help the poor or impoverished. Disharmony and dissent then ensues. It has always been the way.

So, indeed this is a retrograde step on a global level, let alone a national one. Until all countries move towards greater social harmony and integration on a global level to raise equality across the board, problems of one kind or another will always ensue to create yet more problems.

Political decision to ultimately succeed, must like all decisions be born out of love, not self-interest for society, community micro or macro to survive and thrive. Throw off the shackles of self-service, embrace the principles of sacrifice of personal wealth for the spiritual wealth of all. This is the only way forward for true global success at the deepest level. Health is wealth. When society as a whole, is healthy in mind, body and spirit you will truly have a wealthy world. For all will thrive, not just a chosen few."

S.H "So, education must be a central key here. A change to how people are educated to inculcate these sorts of beliefs into the minds of the young to encourage service to others rather than self. Also, ideally teaching of the spiritual principles contained not just in this book – but also many other similar books and from the many other people who espouse these types of teachings. They need to be incorporated into the curriculum of schools globally, to foster such sentiment and belief in our young to help ensure the young are brought up believing and acting in a way to support these beliefs?"

H.S. "Yes, my son."

S.H. "But how can this be further encouraged, as it is politicians around the world who have this power. Though I accept that in many countries, it is the public who vote them in to power?"

H.S. "My son, it is for the populations of your countries to choose wisely, then those politicians who also support change in such directions, to help ensure such educational practices are brought into being. It is only through the greater awakening of society that these changes will become embedded. You are playing your own small part here, by inviting others to read these words to help facilitate change in others and for them to do likewise in their own ways. Both through their own efforts and their gifts which they possess to support such a shift in consciousness towards a greater wisdom of being through sharing your wealth and protecting and looking after your environment on your beautiful planet Earth."

S.H. "What is the difference between love and compassion? That is, if there is any?"

H.S. "My son, love is the embodiment of God in all creation, for all is of God. Nothing would exist without God, for God created all that is. Love is the wisdom behind all of creation. Compassion is the flip-side of love, in as much as it is love in action. Yes, they are much the same. But, compassion is love actuated – love expressed – love in action. Doing what is required out of love at any moment dependent on the situation at hand."

S.H. "So compassion is love in action. Such as if an elderly person falls in the street and someone helps them to get up. That is an example of compassion, or love in action."

H.S. "Yes, for you could feel love for them and you could continue to walk on by for whatever reason. To stop and help them, is a simple example of showing compassion for another."

S.H. "So, by showing compassion we are more fully showing or demonstrating our love for another?"

H.S. "Yes, my son correct."

S.H. "Is there a difference between consciousness and spiritual consciousness, or are they both the same?"

H.S. "Consciousness is if you like, the 'greater' mind shared by God which is shared by all. By definition, as you understand the term 'spiritual': meaning 'of God,' also would mean the same when or as you here refer to the term 'spiritual consciousness'. Then yes, the term means or expresses the same meaning as you are using it here in this context.

Consciousness is the divine mind unlimited by any form known or not known to man. It is the intelligence and awareness incorporated into all creation and that which directs all. It is the intelligence inherent within every atom of being.

You, each of you are the ocean of being, the ocean that creation shares. You are all moving to the remembering of such, each person awakening one by one to this truth. In the collective remembrance of such there will be an ocean of unity of remembrance of the source of your creation, of your creator, that you all share.

You have defined yourselves by your own physical body expressions of yourselves. Yet, you are not confined to that – you never were – it is just that you forgot for a short period of time – who you really are – wonderful creations of unlimited power and love. In your own remembrance of such, share it with the world through your own greater capacity for love and compassion. Practice such each day and teach others through your example of doing such for others as much as you can. Show love and compassion as much as you can for your own true selves inherent within.

Never doubt yourself my son. You have allowed doubt to steal to much of your precious time already. Now that you have rediscovered your own power, refuse to allow your doubt to steal such from you, like the thief in the night, which it but pretends to be. Not just for you, but for all others who allow it to do the same and in so doing allowing it to diminish their own potential from being truly manifest, as God intended it should be for all. Rise up, like lions and roar with your newly discovered voices to show the world that you are here to stay as a new awakened consciousness to heal your Earth from the pain and misery that your mass sleeping state of human consciousness has formerly brought to your planet. Now is the time for the shackles of such to be thrown free so that the full potential of spirit's free can encircle your globe in a true harmony of being so that your lands and people can be freed from the bondage of doubt and ignorance to your true nature of greatness!"

S.H. "This is good. I like it when we get on to a role of prose and inspiration. I feel uplifted on a cold January morning (as it is now as I write). I feel inspired more than ever with my project at hand – 'Awakening to Love book II'. A fresh start, while all around us chaos reigns in the political dramas affecting our various countries, especially in the United Kingdom and the U.S.A.

I am trying to keep my attention away from it all, as much as possible right now. To do otherwise makes me inclined to feel stressed unnecessarily. This is not my path and not my fight. I will leave that to others who feel it to be their calling. While focusing instead on writing these books to help others is more my calling at this time."

H.S. "My son, your enthusiasm for this project fills us with joy and we are here to help answer your questions, to in turn help inspire others to 'awaken to the love that they are'. For to awaken to love' – means to awaken to the love inherent within all. This love is the essence of all creation. Ask to be shown. Ask to be helped, feel this divine love, if you the reader has difficulties. It is only because you dear ones, have cut yourself off from feeling its warm emanations and wisdom from your own selves because of your hurts, pain and disappointment in life.

Simon Herfet

Yet, your pain if you reflect, has been caused often by others through their own indifference to you and their own selves. Through their own ignorance about their own true nature and in turn because of their own attitude and beliefs regarding their own hurt and pain. So, the cycle continues, unless you through forgiveness towards yourselves and towards others is it released you can none of you, move forward into this promised land of unconditional love until you release your hurts, your pain and resentments. Offer them up to God my children embodied of light, surrender your hurts. Know that you are loved and always will be as God's children, that you always will be!"

LOVES LOST HOPE

S.H. "Why is this chapter called 'Loves lost hope?"

H.S "My son, this chapter is called such because the time in which you live is a time of 'transition', if ever there was one. We say this because if you look around you now you will see evidence of this fact. Many people have at this time, in which you find yourselves, have lost 'hope'. Many feel that your world is on a downward spiral into an abyss of negativity and destruction. People have to a great extent lost their sense of 'hope' for a better world. Many have even lost their belief in 'love' for one another to save them from humanity's own self-destruction.

However, to uplift you and their spirits, we would like to remind you all that this 'now' time, is a period of transition for humanity. It is not a time of lost hope in the truest sense. This is because there is much more than just 'hope' in your world for a better future for all.

What you must all remember is that a new generation always succeeds the previous one. This is where your greatest hope lies, for the younger generation to your own is very different, even to your own generation my son. Indeed, so different in fact that they are almost a different race to your own.

Their own priorities in life are so different to all preceding generations in fact. They are a generation that do not wish to receive in the usual sense but wish instead to focus on what they can give unto your world. For in their hearts that is their group purpose for incarnating at this time of 'transition,' my son. For indeed this transition would not occur. In fact, they have come here with the sole purpose to save your world from its many travails. These are the travails of pollution, of endemic crime and bloodshed still in many parts of your world. They have come with their own different soul vibrations to increase the spiritual perspective of your world. They have come to embrace nature and not to destroy it. They have come to create a true organic, holistic environment that your wildlife, nature and fauna of your planet is crying out for to save it from its imminent destruction should your ways not change sufficiently to ensure that this does not happen. So, to ensure its survival a call has been sent out to your heavens to sufficient wise loving and benevolent souls to incarnate and restore peace and harmony to your lands, so that they may be rejuvenated and thrive as they once did. Man living in harmony with nature instead of causing so much destruction as it has until now, my son. Your world is on the cusp of great environmental change. As we have told you previously, your planet is warming. The sun is having a major impact in causing this effect. Its purpose, is to bring areas of land previously protected from destruction by their inhospitable climates into humanity's reach. These environments will become more hospitable and productive to humans as your climate changes. These lands being opened up will bring the protection through the availability of sustainability to humanity for survival through lands made available for greater food production in areas where your soils content has been replenished for thousands of years of being unavailable to you. Temperatures there will be conducive to pleasant life due to their warming. A new vista will be opened to all. Time will heal the wounds of humanity's past destruction and a new ethos of living will ensue. Your teachings will change. Instead of prioritising what you can all get from life, it will be about what you can give to others. Service will be a key element of living in communities conducive to your own health, happiness and survival. Mental illness will largely disappear from human experience as your priorities change in this way. Loves lost 'hope' will return once more, as sharing and caring for each other make a welcome return to your list of priorities, so that community living becomes the norm, instead of the exception.

Cities of light will emerge from the foundations of the great cities which exist now. They will operate differently to now. At the current time your cities are economic hubs of activity. In the future, your cities will still be business centres. The difference: the businesses will focus on community rather than the individual. In so doing, this simple shift of focus alone, will nictitate the change required to ensure all are looked after and nurtured when such nurture is called for. Love will be shared more readily with others at this time of need. For each will see their own interconnectivity through the needs of others, as they themselves address their own needs with each other in harmony and greater self-understanding. This being in the self-realisation that each person is inextricably linked to the other on all levels of their being."

S.H. "So love then will not have lost hope of a better future for all then?"

H.S. "No my son, quite the opposite, as we have just informed you."

S.H. "Oh, thank God for that. The chapter heading before I started to get this information coming through to me, sounded rather negative initially."

H.S. "We understand my son. This book however, is about raising the consciousness of humanity to help to encourage them, others, including your own self too, to change their ways to address the issues, which need addressing now to help to clean up and improve the way, not only how society functions, but how you treat each other. But also, how you treat yourselves, with ever greater self-love and self-compassion.

Remember, as we have told you many times, my son. You are all love. You are all loved. You are indeed, all, the source of that love!"

S.H. "We have just spoken a bit about community living. The implication being that it is much healthier for people, rather than to live isolated. This isolation, most often being felt by those living in cities ironically."

H.S. "Indeed, my son. City living began as community living. As society has changed in many various ways – your social interactions have reduced in no small part due to the many devices available to make your lives easier. However, in turn this has led to a disconnection to others as a result. It is this disconnection from others which has led to so many of society's problems. Yes, you have your electronic devices to connect. However, this is not the same. It is a different connection. It is not direct. It is not a human connection. It is an electronic connection. It takes the heart out of your connection simply because it is not an empathetic heart centred connection. It is a man made one rather than a love centred connection.

When you look a person in the eye a 'divine' connection is made my son. This is a very powerful connection. When you text, email, or speak over a phone this connection does not occur. There is no comparison. One connection is from the soul. The other is soulless in comparison to the former.

Reconnect my son. Spend time in the company of others and make that connection of others with your hearts. Eye to eye, a totally different feeling of connection results. It is true connection, as connection was intended. Face to face you can feel with your hearts i.e. your higher-mind what is troubling to others, in a way you cannot from a place of greater disconnection."

S.II. "Is this a main cause then as I suspect for the very large increase in mental illness of people around our planet now?"

H.S. "Yes, my son it is one cause. Also, this disconnection from nature, from beauty, from others, from your wildlife, from true self-purpose and from a lack of spiritual nurture, love and self-replenishment. This is why so many are seeking for the answer to their problems now in these areas. They know that these areas are lacking. They sense that what they need to heal and feel more balanced within themselves, lie in these areas. People sense that they need to connect with the spirit within their true selves and nature to restore their own sanity when they feel it is lost.

People do not need others to tell them this for they can sense it within themselves. For this wisdom is within all. It is their own self-inherent intelligence of being. God given. They only have to go within whenever they can, to connect with this inner wisdom which all possess and is available to all. It is their own divine connection. Their own inner way to reconnect with their own self-loving inner knowing and wisdom. Here, there lies the answers to all their own questions which they may have. Go within, my own children of love, and seek your answers within your own inner sanctum of your own divine being, for I will meet you there always. I will hold you and address your fears. Always has it been so. All you ever need to do is let go and let God. I love you all remember that my children. I will love you until the end of time which never comes. For time as I have said before does not truly exist.

All that exists is the essence of our true being which is sustained and is shared by all, now and always in "all that is".

PASSED THE EDGE OF DARKNESS

S.H. "What is the edge of darkness?

That sounds a bit ominous to me."

H.S. "My son, what you fear like so many others, is the unknown. The unknown to so many, is the darkness. You fear the unknown because it is that, 'unknown' to you. You do not know or believe perhaps whether you have the capacity to face whatever situation may present itself unto you. For because of the doubt in your own minds you lack the courage, or the self-belief to trust in your divine self that you will be able to deal with whatever presents itself to you.

What you all forget is that you are not dealing with whatever presents itself alone, for there always has been the help of the creator of 'all that is'. The creator with the divine intelligence always inherent within you and at your beckon call will always be available to you all. Surrender my son. Let go and Trust in God. Just as you are doing now, writing these words. You do not know which word precedes the next one until they appear. This is a perfect way for you to demonstrate your trust in the divine. It is because you have asked so many times to be used in this way and because of your trust in the process that you are able to step aside and let these words flow through you. This for the betterment and upliftment of others. Whosoever, chooses to read these 'humble' words. We use the expression 'humble' here because they are presented for and to others in the tone that this information is presented here, as a call, but not an order. Others may choose to accept, or simply choose to decline to accept the message presented here to others. However, the fact that they have been drawn to this book in the first place would indicate an openness to allow these words to wash over themselves."

S.H. "So, I am still none the wiser yet. Do you mean that the 'darkness' is a fear of the unknown for us all, and much of what is required is greater trust and faith in our own divine soul inherent within us all?"

H.S. "Yes, my son. Exactly that. That is what we are trying to express here. That you all let go and allow God through your own trust in the divine-self inherent within you all. You may call it the soul, spirit or atma. Irrespective of the name you use, it is the divine inner knowing and connection to the conscious awareness you all share and are currently all awakening to in greater and greater numbers. This is the age of the 'Great Awakening'. As humanity moves forwards from its slumber in greater and greater numbers, so you will see a ground swell of people of like minds centred on love and compassion, not only for your fellow man, but for all your creation on your planet Earth. The only planet of choice."

S.H. "So, this is about finally conquering our fears or being more in control of such, by surrender and trust within ourselves?"

H.S. "Yes, my son. So much of the pain, difficulty and distrust in your own lives is due to fear, not just of the unknown, but your struggle for survival, be it on the mental, physical or emotional level of being.

If you let go and surrender more as mentioned, so much of the struggle is removed from your minds and emotions making it easier for you to cope physically as well, whatever the issue or challenge you are facing at the time in question. Ask my son. Ask all of you, my children of light. You are connected to this source of being, which is the life force of the loving wisdom resident within you. It is forever listening, but a whisper from your side. Allow its entry to sooth and balm your troubles. Let it ease your anxiety as there is no anxiety unknown, not experienced by the creator of being.

Do not hide from your problem. Like warriors of light that you are – place on your armour of wisdom, the armour of forgiveness for self and others. The armour of compassion. The armour of service to others. Go out into your world knowing that you are always accompanied in your efforts wherever you may find yourselves in your world.

Treat all others as you yourself would wish to be treated in the circumstances that you find yourselves in. Problems that present can always be addressed when you hand them over to the greater wisdom you hold."

S.H. "The inner darkness is so relevant to the inner disconnect so many must be feeling. We disconnect ourselves not just with our thoughts and emotions but also just our preoccupations of many sorts. They take us away from the moment at hand. Though certain activities of course help us to be peaceful and help us to connect to the present more. How come some activities can do this but some have the opposite effect?"

H.S. "The relevant criteria here to answer your question, 'is, does the activity bring you peace?'

If so, it will keep you in the moment. If not, it will take you from it. That is why we keep repeating the message to all – keep on choosing peace. Each time that you feel yourselves being removed from peace – bring yourselves back to peace within your minds.

Say in your own mind each time this occurs – 'I choose peace now' and peace will return to your minds. You need to make this 'mindful' mantra or practice your habit. When peace returns, you will be positioned to make the wisest choice available to you in the moment, if that is required. If not relax in the peace presented to you, my son."

THE SPELL OF MATTER

S.H "I feel that after we have woken up to who you really are i.e. 'a spiritual being having a physical experience, in a material world' – that when you reflect back on how you were before this realisation, that you appreciate more how difficult it can be to 'wake up'.

It is as if there is a spell of matter cast upon us, to keep us asleep to our true nature. Perhaps there is in away?

We are brought up and indoctrinated by our culture, particularly in our largely secular western world that I live in that the sub-total of our being is just mortal skin, flesh and bones! Then we die and that is it!"

H.S. "My son, you are right of course, to an element this is correct and true. It is your own mind which casts the spell to keep you in that place through your beliefs about yourselves. It is through a change in your beliefs which releases you from the spell too. It is only upon releasing yourself from the spell of matter that you realise you were indeed under such a spell. For indeed when you are under the spell of such, you cannot realise for the truth is hidden from you until you awaken to the truth. You are each the seekers of your own truth which is held within you all. It is a process of coming to a remembering about who you really are. When you remember, and assimilate truth into your true being there will be a deep sense of joy, peace and strength which will enthuse your being. You, anyone reaching this realisation will radiate differently to others. People will sense a change – they will not know what is causing the change within the other. That will not matter, for this can only be an individual journey of consciousness into self, into the deepest nature that you and all beings in creation are within themselves. It is only humans at this stage in your evolution who have the capacity to awaken consciously to your true spiritual nature. When you awaken, you will hold the frequency, the key to help unlock this frequency of change for others. A change of consciousness inherent within you all.

The frequency of others, most still being under this spell which you describe, as the spell of matter, is in truth the group frequency of humanity in your communities. When there is a shift at a community level it helps to raise that of the rest of communities. This is an important aspect to community living that few are aware of. As the consciousness can be raised, so it can be lowered too. Keep your company wisely my son. This you know. It is something most commonly taught to your young, but of course it applies to all. Choose your friends wisely. Choose your partners also, wisely."

S.H. "Is there anything else we can do to help humanity from being held down any longer by this spell of matter? Also, is there any element of darkness about the fact it does feel like a 'spell' of sorts?"

H.S. "My son, the spell of which you speak is a self-prophesy of humanity's own thinking. It is not a spell cast by a greater power of any sort, no. It is the group mind of humanity which cast the spell. It is the group mind of humanity which holds the power to break this spell.

This is indeed the stage in which humanity now finds itself. The time of the spell being broken. A time for humanity to be released from the chains of bondage of their thoughts of terror, distress, pain and anxiety from which so many of you suffer so much of your time.

It is due to the bombardment of so much information from sources which holds the frequency of fear rather than peace, that such negativity now engulfs so many of your young, for they are the main ones on the receiving end of such.

Teach them to search for and to look for that which brings them peace rather than distress. Teach them by your own example.

Open your wings and fly now my son. Teach others to fly also – to fly higher into their own higher consciousness and awareness of who they really are. Who they always really were. Who they always will really be. Divine spectrums of God in human form."

S.H. "I know from my own experience, that it is my own fears, my own anxiety and distress which has been caused by a variety of factors, not least my own propensity to have dark negative thoughts about myself. That this pattern was instrumental in holding me back from waking up. However, it was paradoxically, the reason which was also instrumental in helping me to wake up. I knew I had to find my way through my own mental anguish to heal myself. In a way, my own pain was my own gift to myself to help bring me to the point where I now find myself. Not perfectly healed I must add!

However, now I try just to be the witness of whatever arises within my own mind or emotions rather than to identify with them."

H.S. "My son, you have had your own journey and experience to date. Each has their own unique journey of course. A major part of your journey, is through your own souls desire to awaken to itself, in the physical life-embodiment in which you all find yourselves in now. It is the yearning of your soul to awaken within the human you, which drives you to search out his type of information that you are reading right now. It is your cry for freedom from the shackles of the type of feelings and thoughts you spoke of earlier which not only limit your growth towards such, but create pain and suffering not just for yourself, but for those close to you also."

S.H. "So, how else can we connect with the divine soul within?"

H.S. "Each day ask to feel that reconnection. Each day see yourself as a divine soul. Each day see the divine soul within. Speak your truth. Live your truth. Teach your truth. See this in others wherever you can.

Your souls are made from the stuff of love. Your souls are made from the 'stuff' that your universe and your heavens are made from. That 'stuff' is divinity in action. Use your actions now in a more awakened state of awareness – that you are just that. You are all – 'All that is'!"

S.H. "These are all fine inspiring words. But what would you say to the person always in denial of such. The person who does not believe that we all are in truth, divine persons. What would you say to that person i.e. 'the born and bred atheist'?"

H.S. "My son, what can you say? As the saying goes, 'you can take a horse to water but you cannot make it drink'. So, you cannot make another believe. That comes to the individual when they are ready to believe. Each is at their own stage on their own journey through life. Let them go. Let them find their own way. Until they cry out for help. Then help them, as God does always!"

S.H. "I have just read a quote of the Dalai Lama. Part of it mentioned again about being present in the moment. One of the things he said, was because man spends so much of the time worrying in the present moment, that he does not live because of this worry – not being present much either in the present or in the future. Therefore, the person does not live that much of their life as fully as they could have, had they been more present. It has taken me much of my life to learn to be 'present' more in each moment."

H.S. "My son, welcome back to this dialogue here. We have already touched upon this specific, most important aspect of life. That being in the present moment is a challenge for most of humanity. It is a skill which comes with a strong degree of self-realisation of the 'true' self. The true self being the same self, resident and shared within all. The one eternal consciousness which pervades every cell of your being. This self is the eternal witness of you and all. The eternal witness is not affected by any of your thoughts and emotions. Your normal everyday consciousness or mind – the 'egoic' self is affected and it is that with which you all struggle to become master of. You need to learn to be the master of your own thoughts and emotions. By this we do not mean control over them, for this is impossible. What is possible, is your response to them and in so doing, the way that your emotions are affected by them both.

You have the ability through your own inner-self and witness to stand back when thoughts and emotions within you arise –to then be a witness to them and not to engage with them. Simply sit back and observe without judgement or mental intervention. Allow whatever it is to occur and watch. Observe and wait until peace returns within and continue after peace returns. This is a skill which takes constant practice and attention and a degree or level of awareness within you to make this possible. Part of the purpose is to help each individual who reads these words to develop this skill or ability to retain their composure towards such, to enable peace to return each time a storm appears within the individual. To self-calm. Through self-love or attention. To allow the return of calm and peace to the individual's inner world. In so doing, the person whoever it is, will be able more often to reside in the present rather than in a place of fear, anxiety, torment or confusion stealing their own present, their own gift from God from them. Life is short for the purpose of one life-time. Though the soul is eternal. One human life-time is not eternal. Treat the opportunity which life brings to you as a gift and strive for this peace within, so that each of you may be more fully present in your life to love and serve all. This is the true purpose to be more present. To share your wisdom with others and to be able to help others, no longer needing to attend so much of the time to your own issues once they have been resolved through your own efforts as regards your own spiritual growth my son."

S.H. "The Dalai Lama also spoke about our desire (though I think it is often a need rather than a desire) to make money and how our effort to do so can make us ill. Then we spend the money to get well. Then we don't fully live etc. etc. Can you comment on this too please?"

H.S. "My son, making money is a 'choice'. By this we mean, it is in the majority of cases a choice of how you choose to make your living. In the society now upon most of your planet some degree of choice is allowed. What is important here is what choice to take in order to make your living.

Most often the choice is as regards to the financial remuneration paid out for your efforts. If your being does not resonate with your choice of work, sickness can or will result over time. For those of you who have a choice, or have the courage to choose, we would say, follow 'the still small voice within you to guide you to that calling which feels right for you'. This guidance inherent within all can be used for all your decisions, should you choose to do so my son. It is your highest wisdom and should not be ignored. Your detriment will be the result should you choose to ignore your inner voice. This wisdom is there to be used, so do not ignore – follow, seek – ask it for your guidance to be shown when you are unsure and need help to choose the right path through life."

S.H. "Going back to the previous question about trying to remain present as much as you can in the 'now', this is made more difficult for instance, for those with a mental illness. What advice would you give to those people? Or, is it the same? I ask this because I know to remain free from troubling thoughts when they arise, is so difficult."

H.S. "My son, good question. Taken to another level.

The individual so troubled has first to deal with whatever the issues are causing the illness in their mind. Be it physically based, mentally or emotional in its origin. These pains and hurts, fears even, must be dealt with. By dealt with, we mean healed sufficiently within 'self', to allow the individual the space within to practice that which we teach here.

To be able to be sufficiently present with 'self' takes a degree of self-awareness in the first instance. You can be taught or teach yourself to become more self-aware. There are many methods. The best one is to learn meditation. Meditation is the art to become more self-aware. This is because it is about journeying within – the inner-view, yes. When you take this journey, you will confront your own inner fears, thoughts, emotions, pain and sad memories. You need to develop sufficient faith, courage, resilience to go into this space to do the necessary work. Over time if you engage in this work you will reap the benefits that such inner work provides. There is no easy way through this. Your barrier to the pain - is your attitude to the pain. Have a positive approach. Pray, if necessary for the love, courage and support in this regard. God, Great-Spirit, Allah, whatever you wish to name the source of your being. Call out. Pray. Ask and help will come to you, in a multitude of ways possible to you. Be open, for help may come veiled, or in disguise to that which you might expect. But, help will come, of such we can ensure!"

S.H. "Yesterday, I met up with two of my old-school colleagues. One of them, I had not seen for over forty years since leaving school. I couldn't help thinking later about the amount of time that had passed since then. I realised how fast that time had passed. I realised also, despite my own endeavours to practice these teachings for many years how often I personally have struggled to live in the moment and in a way therefore, how much I have missed in those years passed. Ironically, I think I was most present when I was a child and had less to worry about like many others. That on reflection leaves me feeling a bit sad. On a more positive note it makes me more determined though to try even harder to be present in the moment."

H.S. "My son, what is it that you miss the most from your time perceived to have been miss-spent. It is your idea that you missed out on what was going on around you to the fullest degree?

Yet your occupation forced you to be present, by definition of the nature of your work (I was a police-officer). It was in your free time, that you were most preoccupied with your thoughts. You did not miss as much as you think you did. Your preoccupation was not as great as you imagine, for most are preoccupied with one thought or another. Despite this you have worked and endeavoured to free yourself and your mind as much as possible from whatever it was that led to your preoccupation in this way. It was your mental endeavour in this regard which drew your attention to your own spiritual pursuit, to enable yourself to free your own mind from your own prison, created for yourself within your own mind. Though difficult in most respects you have enabled yourself to find the freedom from such.

In other words, my son it was your own chosen journey. Do not be sad, be glad. Be grateful for what you have achieved as a result of your own travails and effort my son."

S.H. "Thank you. I just felt sad for a while that I had spent so much of my life worrying."

H.S. "My son, nothing is wasted. You have turned your worry into a positive. Now you are sat here writing this book with the intention to help others also worry less if they so choose and utilise some of the practices outlined here in this book.

Surrendering to the now. To the divine inherent wisdom within all is all that you need to do. To do this each moment requires a high degree of self-awareness and practice. This takes time to learn, my son."

S.H. "I am sure. So, by being more present in the moment – will this help to free us more from the spell of matter as outlined earlier?"

H.S. "Yes, my son. As we said earlier, it is through your own connection within the present moment that you are in touch with your own true-self. That which all are part of. By being present you are more receptive on all levels of being. As a result, your awareness raises to a higher level of being and you are then more open to receiving information from more levels of your own being. As an example, in the way that you are receiving these words now as you write. This has only come about as you have applied yourself in this way through your own insights, to enable you to connect with the source of this wisdom, in the way that you do now, in total trust and surrender to allow the information to pass through and to your own mind, to be captured here for the benefit of others my son. For others to read at their own leisure. Words to heighten their own levels of spiritual attunement to their own true nature and spiritual connection to their own divine soul latent within themselves. Meditate on these words children of light. Know in the spiritual recess of your own true being that these words will ring true for you also, for you are warriors of light. You each have your own mission here on planet Earth. That mission is to help others in some way. For you are a community of light beings enmeshed in a physical form. But, you are encased within that physical body for only an infinitesimal moment of time in comparison to your true eternal nature. So, worry not about time wasted. Nothing is wasted. All is known and recorded in the mind of God. It can be no other way. For all eyes, are his eyes. All ears, are his

Simon Herfet

ears. You are the creator in motion in this life. So, awaken now to this – your true inheritance of being."

THE COSMIC SHIFT

S.H. "What do you mean by the 'cosmic shift'?"

H.S. "The cosmic shift my son is the change within your own planet's vibration occurring now. This is a shift in the vibration and consciousness of your planet Earth to a higher vibration of being and awareness. The planet on which you all reside has its own awareness and intelligence in a similar way to your own. However, it does not have a sense of 'self'. The planet knows it is a body which sustains many other forms of intelligent life. It provides its many forms of life with sustenance of its being: air, water, earth, wind and fire. All its minerals, soil and other forms of life, are there to enable these myriad life forms to be expressions of God in spiritual form, for no other reason, other than they can. Their source of life however, comes from the loving wisdom behind them all.

It is the loving wisdom of consciousness within them all, that sustains them also to function and live here on your Earth plane. Through the interconnection of being, you are all connected, and the more you realise this the more you will all be able to live in harmony with one another.

Do not see yourselves as separate from any other life form, you are all interdependent. You must learn to look after and safeguard all life forms as much as possible to the best of your ability, for each has a function. Each is a part of the greater whole of which you are all part."

S.H. "So what is the purpose of this cosmic shift of the planet?"

H.S. "The purpose is to assist and embed this greater level of consciousness across the spectrum of being and life forms, to enable a shift in consciousness to flourish on planet Earth to usher in a new age of fruitfulness, peace and harmony on your planet. This time, long prophesised by your elders, has been in the pipeline for a long time. It was always intended to 'be'. For it is part of the cycle of evolution of a planets growth towards self-realisation for all. It is Gods way of waking up too. It is a way for God to wake up even more fully. For as more aspects of God awaken, also each part affects the greater whole. The more parts awake – the more awake is the greater aspect 'of all creation', is awake to the total of its being. also. It is not complicated to understand. If more parts or cells of your body are awake to the essence of being a human body, the more awake the human body becomes. To use an analogy on the micro-level of being."

S.H. "So, is this happening on the micro-level at the same as the universe is waking up to itself?"

H.S. "Yes, my son. But more slowly. Earth and all its inhabitants are like just one cell in a human body at this time. But, in the fullness of time this is the intent of God, to awaken the whole physical universe to its sense of being and awareness of such. The more sentient the being, the more potential that there is for the degree of awareness of 'self'."

S.H. "So, we are all on a journey towards a greater and greater awakening. That is the essence of our life's journey. The deeper purpose behind it all. To keep going and going, deeper and deeper into self-realisation?"

H.S. 'Yes, my son. That is so. You are on a journey in that general direction. The challenge is to stay on course with love always as you guide."

S.H. "Yesterday, I had a good conversation with someone about a variety of topics. One of which was about 'community' and the essence of the meaning of community. I mentioned to him that within this word is not only the word 'unity', but also 'commune', this alluding also to the word communication. Not surprisingly therefore, it reflects the true meaning of 'community'.

H.S. "Yes, my son. Community, in essence, means 'oneness'. This is the inference of the two words you mentioned. It means a coming together of hearts and minds of those individuals who share their lives in some way. Whether, because they live together, or within the same physical place. Peace is the result of community in the true sense. When people live together interdependent of each other they flourish. Their combined efforts towards living and survival ensure that their community not only survives, but flourishes also in harmony, and with love and support shown to each other in times of need and joy. It is natural for one species to enjoy and long for and harbour a need to be surrounded by one's own kin, whether family or others. It is why you are drawn even to others of similar interest, whatever they may be. This is because from such meeting comes the benefit the realisation of feeling that only that shared in a community brings unto you.

A community way of living is your natural way of living. It is the way of living adopted by your species since the beginning of time. It was in part about survival, but also because of the joy it brings to each of you. It fulfils a primal need of feeling a sense of belonging to a group or tribe. So deep is this need, that even in your own ways of living, particularly in your former western world, now your new global economic based world, that this way of living has been lost to a large extent. So much so that disharmony in the individual denied this results, and the community of people in such places is missing this in their lives, and suffering in many ways as a result.

It is more difficult for many to exist and thrive without its benefits which true community living brings.

One of the factors missing because of this lack, is due to the fact that you also do not know others in the same way or depth as you would in a true community. You simply do not spend time together with others, as your ancestors once did. You are all too preoccupied with the requirements and various offerings for your time, that exist now in your modern societies. Be it more often than not, to yours and others detriment of being and wellness.

As a result of this disconnect of living a variety of illnesses ensue amongst many. It will not be until this is addressed that these ills of spirit and mind will be improved.

It is about developing an awareness of such in the first instance and making and the necessary changes to revert to a more organic, holistic, caring way of living not only for self, but others too. Then your true joyful inheritance of community living as it is meant to be will once more return and humanity will once again thrive as it was meant to. This obviously means a simplification in many areas. Your lifestyles have become so complex and time consuming you do not even have time for inner-reflection. Hence why so many do not know how to live in the moment, and are as a consequence so disconnected to their own inner voice, their own spiritual essence within themselves."

S.H. "To me however, this would mean much of society refusing to chase money for their own personal survival. I cannot see that happening, as I think most people would see that as a retrograde step. I can see the many benefits, unless you mean more simply adopting a greater work/life balance."

H.S. "A greater work/life balance is required, as we imply here. It is important to seek balance and harmony within whenever and wherever possible. There is so much in your world which can lead to inner disturbance. None are immune to the possibilities to this occurring. There must be space in your day for inner peace and reflection. To ignore this is an error of judgement. It is food for the spirit, for the soul. You feed and exercise your bodies. You must do the same for your inner bodies of soul and spirit. Their essence is of love and this needs feeding too, for you to thrive and survive also. It is the disconnection from the spiritual self within which ultimately leads to so much suffering. That is why it is so important to love yourself as well as others. You are feeding your inner essence by basking in that love. Whether from yourself or others, each need to feel love, to feel whole and nourished in their existence of being. In the spiritual realm, this is more available as there are no barriers to it reaching your essence – in the physical world there are many. That is why your physical world is so tough. That is why it is such a challenge. Life is a great challenge. But you are all brave souls, or else you would not be here – especially at this time, a time of great change and upheaval, for many changes are on your horizon. Changes your world is ready for now, but was not ready for before now."

S.H. "How can people find that that space within their own lives to communicate more with others and connect more with their own essence and being."

H.S. "My son, by making the time. By making more time for themselves and others too. By withdrawing much of the time that they give to the offerings of others through their electrical devices, which steal their own time, and often their sense of wellbeing. For once you open up to such, you are vulnerable to what will appear to your mind's eye, most often this is to feed the ego rather than the soul of others.

Spend your time on that which feeds your soul, not that which feeds your desires. Your desires are led by your physical needs and desires. Your soul's desires, will only be fed by connecting with those things which bring you deep joy and fulfilment of your heart. Do not be the victims of statement. Do not be the voiceless, choiceless victims of a society which only sees you as vehicles for the embellishment of riches for another. Do not be enticed by the mere trinkets of a consumer society of apathy of true being, for you are not that. Break free from the hypnotic spell of being lost in this material world of possessions, which do not feed your soul but rather suck you dry of your life-force, revealing themselves for what they always were – illusions of something that they never were, my son. Seek instead, the true treasure latent within you all, to enable true joy to enrich all your lives which is based on love for self and others, which re-enables a true community living of caring and sharing with all. Open the channels and the avenues once more, for a deep more meaningful form of communication based on real face to face, heart to heart communication to nourish your own souls."

S.H. "So, we need to get out more. Get off our devices more. Spend more time with others, with one to one heartfelt communication. Helping and sharing with others more?"

H.S. "Yes my son, in essence that is what we mean. Not forgetting the inner contact within yourselves. Your own spirit, your own soul, your own heart. Whether in nature, stillness or meditation. Then there is a greater connection with the 'God' within your own selves, and healing will occur as a result to help you all cope with changes that inevitably occur in each person's life."

S.H "Why is there suddenly the massive rise in the number of people now developing an interest in mindfulness and practising a form of daily meditation. Also, many people are adopting either a vegetarian or vegan diet or even what some might call a 'vegan lifestyle'?

Is this also due to this raising global consciousness within humanity?"

H.S. "Yes, my son. Because you are all connected on a mental level of being, you are more aware of your inner being, your inner nature of feeling. You are all more in touch with your divine-selves. Your own yearning for peace and connection with the divinity within your true selves is paramount at this time. This is not just due to outer disharmony and disconnection with others, only partially so. This is because as the vibration of your planet rises, it affects all that is resident upon her. Because you are all connected at the mental and spiritual level – what one learns – is picked up at the deepest level also by others. This occurs especially within groups of individuals who have a similar resonance of being, they share amongst selves. The driver is a feeling deep within, in part for greater peace and inner harmony. This is driven in part for the global desire, for global peace and harmony. This has to start within the individual, before it can spread out to the macrocosm.

Mindfulness begins with the individual person's awareness growing towards greater clarity, of both thought and feeling, and a greater desire to be present.

The desire or need for meditation, is driven by the spiritual need for inner calm and an inner spiritual connection to the divine within 'oneself'.

The move towards either vegetarianism or to adopting a vegan diet - in other words, abstaining mainly from meat and dairy produce, is due to a greater resonance of being within, and feeling a greater connection with the divine within. This does not infer superiority over others, merely a choice of changing one's habits because of feeling different within, to how one once did previously.

The person is more in touch with their inner-self. They feel happier healthier within than they once did, because of such practise.

We must not forget here either, the connection to exercise and health and happiness. Exercise, is a prerequisite to obtaining joy through a healthy body. You do not need a healthy body to feel joy. But, you are more likely to feel such when the body is performing nearer it's optimum level of being, whilst in your physical existence here on Earth."

S.H. "We spoke about mindfulness previously. Can you recap a bit more about the essence of mindfulness and how to practise it?"

H.S. "Mindfulness my son, it is the ability to be able to focus in any given moment on all that is present in the moment within. It is the ability to be aware of your thoughts and feelings and actions in each moment. Just being the observer of such, in non-judgement of them. The aim being to heal that which is dissonant with the true self, or not in true harmony with inner being. Through practise and inner training by such method, the aim being to bring thoughts and feelings back into alignment with a feeling of peace within oneself."

S.H. "And how would you describe meditation and the difference between mindfulness and meditation?

To me they are quite similar. The former being easier to adopt while going about your everyday activities."

H.S. "Indeed my son. Though this does not have to be the case, it is the norm. Meditation, is the practise of going within to connect with the inner witness through stillness.

Mindfulness is the practise of self-observation of thoughts and feelings at any time whether in meditation or any other activity. Meditation is mindfulness in stillness.

Mindfulness, is meditation whilst active if you like. Meditation is easier in many ways because of the lack of outer distraction."

S.H. "Is the purpose of meditation to connect with our spirit within or to help decrease stress?"

H.S. "There is no purpose other than to connect with the peace and stillness within you all. Making that connection as a by-product brings through peace – a greater sense of divinity within oneself and therefore helps the body and mind feel in a calmer state of being. This is beneficial to most persons. We say most, because for some people, this state, because they are so unused to it, brings up their own fears which they spend so much time trying to run away from. However, they only arise because of the inherent need for them to be dealt with, to allow a healing to occur within said individual, my son."

S.H. "Thank you. So, these are all very good ways, or methods, to reconnect with the divine soul within, are they not?

What other ways can this also be done?"

H.S. "By feeling as much love within yourself, for self and others. By practising what you preach here, my son. By loving all and serving all, wherever possible. Each person has their own god given gift to share with the world to help others. Just do this as best you can, throughout as much of your life as you can, my son. Until your last day of life, if possible, my son. This does not mean never to rest or stop doing what you enjoy, whether alone or with others. We mean here within reason. As part of your daily practice, be kind, loving and helpful as much as you can to others. Help others smile, share your peace, share your wisdom, share your love!"

RETURN FROM THE VOID

S.H. "What do you mean by return from the void?"

H.S. "My son, for eons of time humanity, in general, has lived in a spiritual void – a disconnection with the truth within yourselves. The spiritual dimension of being is easily accessible while in the human body, as long as the individual is open to love through their heart and soul. Humanity suffers a disconnection through their beliefs, and a disconnection in their hearts through many other emotions as well as fear – hatred, envy, non-forgiveness, jealousy, resentment, hurt, emotional pain of many sorts, for many reasons. Also, through an arrogance of self-importance. A belief that one's self is greater or more important than another. Each is equal in the eyes of God – no matter colour, creed, or sex. You are equal and loved by God. Accept yourselves. Accept your failings. You are loved irrespective. You are all forgiven. Follow that light and direction within your hearts."

S.H. "So, the void you refer to, is the inner emptiness that so many feel, despite often an abundance of material wealth and prosperity."

H.S. "Yes my son. Material wealth is meaningless to the spirit within. It is not eternal. Only the riches of the soul are eternal. These are learnt through loving action towards others only. You cannot buy kindness. You have to earn it through your own practice and action. That is why we keep on saying 'love all. Serve all.'"

S.H. "So, to return from that place of emptiness, that so many feel, we simply have to love and help others as much as we can. Including loving ourselves, forgiving ourselves for our wrongs?"

H.S. "Yes, my son. This makes it sound very easy, when in truth so many find this very difficult. It is difficult for them, not because they are bad, simply that they have got into bad habits, or rather habits which do not serve themselves well, or others. Those are mental habits which don't serve, physical habits, emotional habits which can be detrimental to self and others.

Pray for help with these. Whichever ones beset you. Whichever ones steal your peace. Love them. Let them go. Thank them for that which they have taught you.

Release them gently. Be gentle with yourselves. Let them fly away. Invite in this sweet replacement – love, light and laughter.

These emotions will raise you, will raise not only your spirits and sense of wellness, but will raise the same qualities in those other persons around and close to you, both in your families and communities."

S.H. "Basically then, to return from the void – the more we can live in the 'power of now', the 'present', the more we can be present there in our minds, as much as possible, then the more potential we will have to keep returning from that void. That abyss of emptiness within ourselves that so many feel for so much of their time, in their lives?"

H.S. "Yes, my son correct. Yet that is yours and their challenge, each day. Having the self-awareness to remember to keep coming back to that moment. This moment is all about your own awareness and ability to do such. This is why meditation is so beneficial. It teaches you how to do this yourself, in your own way. This is the prime purpose of meditation. It helps you to return to the 'now' moment over and over again.

When you are in the present moment '<u>you are sitting at the feet of God</u>' – in your power – connected to the divine wisdom inherent within you all."

S.H. "And when we are so present, with the gift of the 'present', we set ourselves free from our troubles whatever they may be. We choose peace over turmoil or worry, or whatever is playing on our minds. When we reconnect we access the divine intuitive, inherent wisdom within our souls which can lead us out of our predicaments if we allow it too. If we listen to that still small voice within us all. To help guide us through our difficulties."

H.S. "Yes, my son. Well said. You do not need me. You are up and running with this dialogue. Ha! "

S.H. "No, don't leave me. I don't mean to steal your thunder. Ha, ha."

H.S. "Yes, my son, we allow of course, you to express your own inherent wisdom, also. There is no dividing line as such when you are attuned in this way. This information is accessed by yourself through the conduit of your own being. Your own soul makes its own connection with your own higher aspect of the group soul to which you belong on a vibrational level of being, which is very difficult to put into your words, as it is not similar in any way to your life here in the physical form. There is no limitation of being on the vibrational level of being. The opposite to your physical level of life expression in the human form. Yet there is still the ability latent within all to connect with this higher level of self-expression, and is this level with which you connect to with these words here, within this open dialogue for all to see. Within the words, within their frequency of use here is a key- code of potential awakening for the reader if the words resonate, to stir and generate an awakening within their own soul's mind, towards this higher awareness level of being and expressing towards others while in the human vehicle or body for the soul.

Open your hearts, your souls to this divine loving potential within you all. Allow the joy and love to enter your hearts in each moment. Do not deny it access there because of a false belief or self-pride that you are already enough. Because until you allow God into your own sacred space you are not fully alive until God has filled it, for you are 'God's' expression being here in this human form. God waiting all the while for your race to awaken in unity of this realisation so that Gods plan of a continuum of peace and prosperity may be revealed for all to enjoy, not just a few. The age of Aquarius is upon you now. Rejoice."

THE DIVINE SOUL WITHIN

S.H. "Sometimes, I struggle to keep a feeling of connection with my own soul and intuition due to my own worries, fears and disappointments. I allow these thoughts and feelings, too often to steal me away from the present moment, where I know peace can be found. Sometimes not surprisingly, I get impatient with myself when this happens. The irony being the frustration caused is just another feeling or emotion to keep me from being truly present. I feel that I have wasted so much of my life by not being fully present. Mainly, because of my own worry and fears or by one mental obsession or another. I am much better than I once was, but I still have some way to go to achieve my full objective in this regard."

H.S. "My son, do not be so judgemental of yourself. You are not perfect yet in terms of your own personal development. Accept this fact. Allow whatever it is that troubles your own mind. Do not try to run away, or escape it. Sit with it. Allow the storms to come and go, as they surely will. While you are in the human body these feelings are a natural part of the human experience. You cannot stop them from arising. You can only allow and watch them until they subside – remembering always that they are not you! They simply pass through you – if you allow them to do so. When you pay them attention without involvement, they will dissipate more readily. However, if you react rather than simply observe them you will feed and energise them and keep them within your experience longer. Therefore, being unable to be fully present until they are released from your mind. Be their 'witness' only, as much as possible, rather than involve yourself with, or try to free your mind or self of such unwanted thoughts or feelings."

S.H. "This is not always easy to do especially if there is a feeling of fear or anxiety which accompanies the thoughts that sometimes arise. This is when I find it especially difficult."

H.S. "My son, these are old thought patterns of which you speak. Are they not?"

S.H. "Yes, they are."

H.S. "And you have noticed the pattern of how they return to you at times of nervousness, whether through excitement or fear?"

S.H. "Yes, I have."

H.S. "This is because such thoughts were originally born out of such feelings and you associate subconsciously, the feelings with these types of repetitive thoughts. You have however, your own series of methods to deal with these, when they occur. Have you not?"

S.H. "Yes, I have."

H.S. "You get frustrated when these thoughts return having had a break from them. Remember, that you have grown stronger and wiser. Know that the thoughts will pass. Focus on peace – as you do. Allow peace each time they occur to take precedence and allow peace and calm to return.

Adopt the same method within yourself to deal with emotions which counter those of peace. Simply that my son."

S.H. "Thank you. I will."

H.S. "My son, it is the mind which acts like a thief in the night, which steals the present moment from you – but only if you allow it! In each moment, you have the choice to allow it to do so. But again, only if you allow it to. Remember each power within you, to keep your connection with the divine soul within you functioning in peace and harmony with your human-self. By this we really mean the human condition of thinking and feeling through the emotions. Remember as we told you in the previous volume of this series of books. Your emotions are like the lake surface, and thoughts are like pebbles tossed into the water. The ripples are like the emotions which ensue across its surface. In time, they stop. Wait and allow peace to return in a place of patience within. All of these practices take a period of time to learn. Until eventually, mastery of them results. For some this can take lifetimes, my son. Be patient with yourself. Keep returning to that source within. This may seem a repetitive process to deal with this issue. However, this cause is equally repetitive. Not surprisingly, the way to counter the symptoms of disharmony also require repetitive behaviour to bring you back and return you to that altered place within. This my son is the process of how to reconnect with the divine soul within by allowing, by opening up and making a space within yourself. A sacred space to feel that peace and love within yourself."

S.H. "How do we deal with disappointment when something we hoped would happen, does not seem to be happening. Is it because we allowed ourselves to think or believe it would happen?"

H.S. "My son, your expectation or hope is the motivation for that of which you speak here. What we would say to you at this time is that you are still at a very early stage with your project at hand. It is like a book. You are only part way through the book and feel disappointed with it so far. Yet, you have not finished it – there is more to come. You yourself will normally persist to the end. So, it is with this process. Do not allow yourself to be disappointed, for it is an early stage of the process and there is much still to be revealed to occur, to happen, to surprise you! Do not pre-empt it. Allow it to unfold fully my son."

S.H. "I hear what you are saying. Thank you for your advice here."

S.H. "Since I was a teenager, I have been on my own quest in search of wisdom, and ultimately what I felt to be some of the answers to some of the secrets surrounding life. My desire now is to help others to find some of these answers for themselves, also on the pathless land to their own truth."

H.S. "So, it is my son, and yet it is also one of many paths all leading to the same centre, the same truth for all. That is the one divine truth – that all are divine emanations of a spiritual force far greater than your own perception of self. You are vast magnificent emanations of light and love. You are conscious awareness permeating even the light that shines upon your planet. There is nothing that you are not a part of. You are 'all that is'. Yet, you see yourself as separate creatures of habit. Your own prison is the prison you each build with your own minds. It is within each – your own capacity also to open your own prison gates, back to freedom, to the realisation of truth of who you really are. You are the divine soul, while still connected to all the other divine manifestations of love. Whatever their form, whatever the space they occupy in your universe, manifest or unmanifest.

Your access point to 'all that is' – is through an open heart of loving acceptance to whatever comes into your life. Once having accepted it, then change it if it is not to your liking – but it is through the initial acceptance that subsequent change can occur. Acceptance is the gateway to change. Without acceptance, you will be stuck in the inertia caused by non-acceptance. This non-acceptance is a denial of the greater truth of who you really are. It is because of an acceptance of an erroneous belief that you are lent to, which you do not allow acceptance to access to build the bridge to your freedom of thought and mind. It is the acceptance which opens the prison gate and allows you to escape back to the freedom from which you came. This is the freedom of the great spirit which animates all souls. It is the wisdom of love which flies on the wing beside you always, as close to you as your breath, and beyond. It is the charisma of your yearning for you soul's access point to this gateway of greater being which drives you on ever forward, on your journey towards greater truth, harmony and peace within yourself and within the world around you. If you but emanate peace in each moment, life will open up to you in the way you deserve it to do so and enable you to fulfil your ambition to share this knowledge with as many others as is possible."

THE CHANGE IS HERE NOW

S.H. "Is it possible to live in a global community of oneness?

Will all people one day really wake up to the fact that we are all connected and then live accordingly, in the spirit of oneness?"

H.S. "My son, this is humanity's choice. Do you each choose to live in loving acknowledgement of the truth of your being, or do prefer to live in ignorance of the truth that has always surrounded you?

To awaken is a painless procedure. To stay asleep to truth is the opposite. It is a painful fate. It is the path out of amnesia open to all that is within your own selves. To delay your awakening though will not be possible when you are surrounded by others who are awake to the divine consciousness which circles you all. This is because of your interconnection of being, one cannot live in isolation of divine consciousness and so my son, it cannot but pervade your being like rain upon your Earth. When the family of humanity chooses this path, the result is inevitable. Humanity has chosen this higher path now my son, be assured of this. This is the reason now for so much of the positive change you see around you, despite the myopic distortion of much of your media. Open your eyes to all that is good and positive which is also being lovingly shared, my son. Most of your younger generations have arrived now to this calling as agents of change, to usher in a new era, of a liquid flow from one consciousness state in a place of fear, to a new era free from the shackles of fear which have kept so many trapped for so long in the belief of an isolation of being. You are not existing any longer in a world of separation, you are moving now quicker and quicker towards a new world of a shared unity. A shared unity of connected loving divine intelligence. This intelligence has been birthed in your human form now to sweep away all that is old and no longer serves your race. Instead, to replace such, to rebirth your Earth, your lands. This will take a little time, but it is a time already settling into your minds and hearts as we speak, forming new roots of inter-connected thought in the still spaces which were left for this purpose. To enable your brains to function at the level and to the degree that they were intended to function. As divine agents of change and co-creation with the creator of your being to build a new earth, a new heaven, to move forwards towards this greater understanding of your divine purpose here on this planet now."

S.H. "Even though I have had to struggle for much of my life with my own anxiety, I have had the good fortune I believe, in being blessed with resilience of character. This has helped me push through my difficulties. My courage has always been my companion in times of difficulty. I realise more each day about the power of positive thought. The power of keeping a positive mental attitude. Exercise for me too has also been great to keep my mental attitude positive. When I slacken off from my exercise routine (I like to cycle), I notice a dip in my positivity levels. Also, I have noticed the importance of a healthy diet. My wife has helped me a lot to get back into exercising regularly and she also has been a great advisor regarding my diet. I am sharing these facts here also just to show that these things have also helped me with my own wellbeing."

H.S. "My son, thank you for sharing this information here. Many will be able to identify with the issues that you address here and realise the importance of them all.

If we take positive attitude to wellbeing first:

Yes, of course and not surprisingly, the importance of such is paramount. In essence, you are each the architects and builders of your own lives. This takes place in each moment. In each moment, your actions are dictated by the thoughts and feelings that you have about yourselves and within yourselves. These thoughts and feelings therefore have a direct influence on how you choose to spend your time and what you will or will not achieve with your own lives. Your minds are like the director for you own life's movie in which you appear i.e. your own life experience. It stands to reason that fear and doubt will hold you back. Positive thoughts of self-belief and trust without doubt will encourage you forward. Fear will imprison your actions. Love will help you flower towards your own self-achievement in life.

The power of your mind has also, a direct influence on the direct health of your physical body. If you believe yourself, that you will be well, you will be well. If you believe yourself, to be ill, you will become ill in time.

Focus on wellness. Focus on wellness always. In all way's possible. See your body as healthy. See your mind as healthy. See your life as healthy. See your relationship as healthy. See your family as healthy. See your country as healthy. See your world as healthy. By this we mean to focus only on all that is well and healthy with all these dimensions of life around you. Focus on all that is good and positive. Uplift yourselves. Uplift others with your messages of love and hope. Hope creates a better world for all."

S.H. "Thank you. Today, I realised that my fear or anxiety was not really about anything in particular, other than negative thinking. That I needed once again to regain more positivity in my attitude towards my own life. Also, to get back out on my bicycle and do more vigorous exercise to help raise my positivity levels."

H.S. "My son, you have your own methods which help you. Many people are helped in a similar way for a similar reason. You find your own sense of purpose also helps to sustain your momentum. Each person's sense of purpose is different too, dependant on their own calling to help others.

You are expressing your own gift's here, in part by writing these words, to help to uplift and inspire others to awaken to their spiritual essence and to live more accordingly to such an awakening. As your awareness is raised and that of others, one of the main benefits is a greater thoughtfulness of other people's issues and the issues for your world, for your planet. Your planet is your home while here on Earth. The rest of creation which shares your Earth, is dependent on its survival through harmony of living by all life forms. As one suffers, then there will always be a detrimental effect on the greater bio-system of your planet. You are all inter-dependant on the other. All of life is interconnected.

If you poison one species of life to benefit yourselves, you will only but poison yourselves as a way of paying the price for your foolish actions. You cannot poison your world to prosperity. You cannot deplete your oceans without failing to see the detrimental effect on the life which thrives within them. You cannot continue to rape and pillage your lands without raping and pillaging the soul of humanity.

You must live in loving awareness towards all of life around you, which is but the co-creator of all staring back into your own eyes. Even the insect which eats your crops is you – looking back at yourself wanting to be fed. Not wanting to be fed a poisonous chemical, an insecticide, herbicide or pesticide, which in turn poisons your own family. The human family.

Go my son, share your information with others. To those drawn to these words of peace. May each person then for once obey the still small voice within themselves, whispering like a voice on the wind to the hearts, which for so long refused to listen to the message of life."

S.H. "Meditation and mindfulness is very much the zeitgeist now. It seems to help a lot of anxious and stressed people cope with various problems in their lives. I do think that meditation helps greatly to improve our capacity to be more aware of our thoughts and feelings which is a very beneficial skill to acquire in our lives. Is there a right or wrong way to practice meditation, or being 'mindful'?"

H.S. "No, my son. They are both similar practices, be it the former is passive the later more active. Both share the same element of inviting the 'witness' that you are and that you each possess, to be present as far as possible, to be aware of your being and to address accordingly that which needs to be addressed in the right way for you in each moment that you can be aware of."

S.H. "Ways to teach us to raise our self-awareness to the highest level which we are capable in each moment.?"

H.S. "Yes, my son in each moment that you are able to do so. Your life is such, that this will not be reasonably practicable always. But rather in each moment that you can train yourself to do so. It is these types of practices that help you to build this inner communion with your spirit or your soul which share the witness within you. The divine consciousness shared by all and connected to all that is the source of the witness within you. Your consciousness is never still, it is always flowing, always moving, alive. It is eternal not just in its presence, but also in its knowing. It is eternal knowing and feeling, feeding from an ocean of love which sustains it. It is the reason that humanity feel the great need for love to be experienced for their own survival in the human form. You can in each moment experience this love within yourselves. Allow it. Feel it. Within your own heart, it resides always. All you have to do is to remember to open the door of your heart each time you find it closed!"

S.H. "Today, I had a different experience to any I have had before during a meditation and I have meditated daily for over thirty years now.

In my own meditation, I deliberately faced my own death in a different way. I imagined myself meditating next to my own dead body to watch my emotions at the experience. What I discovered from doing this, was how detached I felt from my own dead physical body. This was because in my imagining of the situation, I sensed the eternal nature of my consciousness – my own awareness present within my soul. That in fact that is what I was left with. Reassured by this feeling I could feel emotionally detached from my physical body and ready and free to move on, were this to be a real situation.

This self-imposed experience was my own deliberate use of my own imagination, its purpose being to help me to release more of my own fears that I have surrounding illness and death. To help free me from such so that I can feel lighter - more carefree in my life which remains. I do feel this somewhat now. I hope that this feeling continues. I still as mentioned, struggle at times with feelings of anxiety and sometimes feel that it has been a handicap to my own progression in various areas of my own life. However, it has also taught me much."

H.S. "Indeed my son. You have reached a point in your own spiritual progression to be able to face such eventualities. To face one's own death takes not only courage, but the serenity to face one's own fate, one's own death which lies before you all. It is the fear of death ultimately, which has been the source of so many of your fears which surround illness.

By facing through your imagination, your own death you are facing such fears. Through this experiential situation, you are allowing your higher wisdom to take you by the hand across the threshold of death, which must be faced by all eventually. Yet, indeed death has no bite. No sting. It is an illusion of ending – of life ending – for life does not end of course. Life continues merely in a different form. You are not a victim of death. Yes, the body dies. The mind, as you know it, dies. But the perfect pristine conscious awareness that you all are, that you all share goes on. Unbroken, no different to before death. That sense of being within you will continue. That depth of aliveness is not dulled, but will be more clear. Your thought and pains will no longer plague you in the same way. You will feel a sense of love never experienced in your human life experience. A sense of safety previously unknown in the physical life.

You have gained much, another subtle shift of consciousness my son, by facing your fears in this way. It is an ongoing incremental journey, my son. All is beneficial in this regard, as it helps you move forwards with greater clarity and lightness in your being, my son. More able to share your experiences with the world whilst here, my son."

S.H. "I do not wish this to appear as a solemn practice to imagine such a thing, for me it is simply being able to face a fear, having gone beyond the fear. For in so doing this, on this day, I felt no fear. I was surprisingly unattached to my own body as I imagined it lying there motionless – devoid of life, because I knew it was not me. That was what was so freeing about the visualisation. Some might say that is because it was just imagination, but to me the experience felt real."

H.S. "Yes, my son. In the mind, to the mind it was real. The mind cannot discern between imaginary and real on that level of consciousness. Your soul, however, does know the difference. During your meditation's your soul has control, for it is the witness to that which was occurring."

S.H. "Yes, that is how it felt, as could best be described in words. What I found most striking is that in all the years and all the hours I had meditated previously, I had never deliberately imagined such a scenario about myself. Maybe, simply because I was too scared. Not ready or wanting to do it."

H.S. "Precisely my son. That is the reason. Rejoice in your willing awareness, not only to have the courage to do so, but with the detachment that you now possess. This indicative of how far you have come with your own spiritual growth and self-awareness."

S.H. "How can the average person then overcome their own fears of such similar things?"

H.S. "By doing as you have done my son. By facing their own fears and asking for help each day in their own prayers. God, Allah, Great-Spirit, call it what you will, that all pervasive spiritual loving wisdom, within and without which holds all of creation in its embrace – holds you all.

Take its hand and it will lead you to your own freedom and salvation from those emotions which hold you in their shackles whether they be guilt or any other emotional pain. Throw them off my son, throw them off, people reading these words. In each moment, you have the freedom to set yourselves free from the prison bars of your mind and your emotions you have created within yourselves.

Create a new world outside and within yourselves to access more freely the divine loving you meant to express in everyday actions, as you live here on this magnificent world with others, all your brothers and sisters in light communion."

S.H. "How does someone who is really frightened or anxious. Someone who is even mentally ill, face these fears then?"

H.S. "My son, by doing just that – facing them. Not trying to avoid them. Digging deep into their own spiritual reserves of courage, and as much as possible with their heart open. So, eventually the feelings of love will over-ride fear as they surely will in time. They must learn to replace their fear with their own love inherent within themselves. Love will conquer all. It may be a cliché, but it is true none the less. Love has a great power many times greater than fear. This is because life springs only from love. Deaths come from fear. When you conquer your fear of death, then more love will be expressed by the individual, for less fear will be present to block its path towards expression from the individual my son."

THE SPIRITUAL DIGITAL REVOLUTION

S.H. "We are now more connected than ever before. I know that so many people, especially young people get obsessed with their electronic devices so often, and are not as engaged in conversation perhaps as they were in the past. Yet, there is no denying, that we connect with many more people all around the world. There are obviously many positive elements due to this which will help many people through sharing information so freely and easily."

H.S. "Yes, my son. Your world is now open in a way it was not previously. Information can be shared and dependent on the intent and purpose of the information shared, so, it will be directly proportional to the outcome of that sharing. What must be uppermost in the mind of the individual so sharing, must be their intent and purpose for that which they share. If the intention is to help others in some way, then this will generally be beneficial to others and advantageous to their lives in general in turn. Yes, continue with your informational sharing. If, however, that which you share is shared with a negative intention – so, if behind the sharing was to in any way attempt to cause suffering to another of any species, whether emotional, spiritual, or physical, then such an action of sharing will not benefit your society or your planet.

So, intention of purpose is the question you must try to always ask yourself before you share information – is the information for the benefit and upliftment of others? Or, do I wish in some way to seek malice towards another for whatever purpose?

Your digital world through your electronic devices of communication, whatever form they take are a gift to humanity if used wisely. Like words, they can hurt others. Even in some instances lead to the death of others. In the worst instance, if used incorrectly they can lead to wars. Just as your televisions and even radios which you have had access to for many years could disseminate information which could spread infraction and hatred among populations, so, can your digital media. Do not underestimate its power – children of light when you use these devices, use them with fore-thought and good intent always. Allow and use them as tools to spread love and intelligent information to benefit and help others raise their own living standards and consciousness."

S.H. "How about the fears of parents about their children spending too much time on smart phones and computers etc.?"

H.S. "My son, while in the hands of children this is the responsibility of parents to 'police' their child's use to make sure they do not overindulge in its use and that they view only that which is suitable for their age."

S.H "I often hear other adults say that because such devices are such a recent invention, that we just do not know what the future effects of the devices will hold in store for the future development and wellbeing of young people, such as teenagers for example."

H.S. "It is as previously stated. This will depend on the amount of time and the purpose which they are used for by the person in question. It is common sense. If an individual of any age over uses these devices and avoids human contact as a consequence, then their own social skills will diminish also accordingly. Balance in all things my son. Remember also to exercise in nature. Healthy body – healthy mind as the saying goes my son, is still congruent advice for all. Nature holds its own psychological healing properties and the more humans can immerse themselves in the balance and peace that nature provides so readily and freely, the result will always be of great benefit to those who seek its solace my son."

S.H. "So, how does this digital age intersect as a spiritual revolution. Is it just through being a readily available global platform to assist the sharing of all kinds of information."

H.S. "Yes, that is so primarily, my son. But it is the speed at which the information can be shared as instantaneously, other than by natural means. The revolution comes about not just for the speed of such but for the ready availability of the technology with so many who so recent in your past did not have the ready access to such equipment and technology. They did not have either the financial or practicable means to be able to do so. Now they do.

However, the speed of the transfer of the information even by such methods as are available to so many now by digital or electronic means, these methods are still so vastly inferior to the subtle methods of information sharing available that operate on the frequency of light through the direct lattice and matrix which consciousness provides, the intersection of loving conscious awareness shared by all at the spiritual level. Your technology for all its gifts is so vastly inferior to the potential and speed of information available to the spirit within. This information is carried on the currents of love which are shared on the gentle subtle frequencies of love and accessed by the higher mind resident in the heart of each human.

As your human consciousness expands into the awareness shared at this level, so, will the brain of humanity continue the expansion in its development towards this purpose, you will see – be it in your distant future that even these digital electronic devices will one day also appear prehistoric in their format and their use. They are precursors of change. They will lead the way to this even greater means of informational sharing that is only possible on the currents of love. Only information that is resonant with such will be shared and available. Only those beings of sufficient love, light, intelligence and consciousness will evolve to this stage and level of being and informational sharing. This however is the direction in which your race is moving, heading towards. This is still someway off in your race's future my son. However, it will come, it will arrive my son. For destiny's child waits in the wings of humanity's future. Your future selves whisper to you all and encourage you forward on your journey to a greater and greater awareness of your true self. The ocean of your being shared by all in a unity of oneness of spiritual intelligence far surpassing the degree and level at which humanity still functions.

Your future selves call out to you now with their arms held open wide to embrace you into the future that awaits you all where life

Simon Herfet

enhancing information is shared by all on the currents of love at the speed of light which illuminate you all in your truth and being."

TRUST IN LOVE AND RELINQUISH FEAR

S.H. "If you pay attention to the media at this present time it is very easy to be afraid of what is happening on our planet right now, what with politics, the destruction of so much of our environment, species threatened with extinction due to a variety of factors, including the overuse of various chemicals such as pesticides etc. Not to mention the human causes adding to global warming. How do we relinquish our fears with regards to such topics being of great importance to us all?"

H.S. "My son, we have told you many times before – to trust, to surrender to the divinity held by all. This does not imply doing nothing. Trust takes faith and belief in the divine inherent goodness in all creation and that everything happens for a good reason. Although the destiny of mankind is in part in the hands of mankind, it is also held in God's hands too.

God controls all, knows all and sees all. Nothing escapes the eyes, or mind of God. Nothing is out of Gods control. However, God allows, God accepts humanity and its folly's. Humanity must learn from its own mistakes including those towards natures wellbeing. This is of course, because it also affects humanity's wellbeing.

The chemicals of which you speak are detrimental to the wellbeing of nature and humanity. However, humanity will become more aware of the use of such chemicals and eradicate their use in full time. They are used out of ignorance largely to provide more food in the way of crops and of course from the financial aspect to which they provide to all working to produce them. These chemicals also produce a great deal of wealth too for a few, at the great expense to the health of many. Most of the allergies now suffered by humans in recent years reflects the use of such chemicals. Some being ingested, some being digested causing harm to the body. This is not found as a surprise as their intention for use, is the purpose to kill and eradicate other life forms.

You also being life forms, will be affected in a similar way to the wildlife they are intended to prevent damaging and consuming your crops.

In the fullness of time your younger generations will take the helms of power in business, finance and politics to use their more enlightened knowledge of opinion to ensure the proper changes are made to eliminate their use. This will be to great benefit of course to all life forms. Your food production will become more sustainable towards your planets resources. Life will start to reflourish where it has become impoverished, and your lands and waterways, including oceans will be returned to their former glory teaming with the life they were intended for. Humanity will learn to live side by side with nature including the animal kingdom, as your consciousness raises, through your joint greater awareness of the interconnectivity of all life. Your spiritual connection to all of life will flourish anew, as you learn the mistakes of old so that they are not repeated.

Your digital social network of informational sharing of these truths will play a large part in this, as it will make the dissemination of falsification and disinformation more difficult. You will all learn to see through 'fake' news my son."

S.H. "So, sharing this news whether good or bad, if its intention is to raise awareness of harm that certain practices cause, such as the seriously detrimental effect of insecticide on the global population of these creatures – is by definition because we can so quickly and easily bring these issues to the attention of the public."

H.S. "Yes, my son. Correct."

S.H. "I like many others, obviously want to help raise awareness surrounding these issues. The fact that many farmers feel trapped by the nature of their communities to keep quiet about these facts to protect their own livelihoods, as they do not know how else to deal with the issues – including being in financial debt to organisations connected to these agro-chemical industries which produce these chemical products. Some are, I know, trying to adopt a more organic approach to their farming practices. Global government, as with many other issues need to work in unison – in unity – to adopt a global radical approach, to outlaw their use to protect all concerned."

H.S. "My son, if you feel this is your calling then follow your heart in doing so. You are already helping to spread this message by writing about it here in this book. You are raising awareness of this issue!"

S.H. "Yes, I know. An article which I read yesterday, in a national newspaper, reported that by the end of this century, if we continue using these chemicals at the rate we are now, then there will be no insects left on the planet. This made me feel like crying. It is easy to feel helpless. You are right, we have a lot of power, even just through our ability to share this information with others in so many ways now."

H.S. "Information is power, my son. Use your information wisely, this is a very important issue. As we have previously said, your world faces many great changes and upheavals for many at this time. You live on shifting sands of being. There is great fluidity and transition in humanity's joint thinking right now.

Less materialism, more spirituality is required. By this we mean, more looking within for completeness, joy and satisfaction with life and being. The more you can relinquish fear, the more room you make for love to animate and energise your very being in existence.

Your existence as you have known it in your short life-time, is on the cusp of great dramatic change never seen before in your Earths history. Continents will rise. Continents will fall my son. Oceans will Shift. Sea's will rise. Lands once unavailable, will become available for human occupation and other life forms will follow.

Your spiritual core, your spiritual centre of being is what will endeavour the success and survival of those who follow you my son, in this lifetime. Part of your mission and purpose is to pass on these words to others who read them, so that they can psychologically prepare for what lies ahead of them. You are a brave soul, my son, encourage others to face their own fears and plough on forwards trusting in the actions of the creator- God you all share."

S.H. "So, simply, the more we can enable ourselves to trust in the divine wisdom, love and power inherent and available in all of us, the more that we will be able to relinquish or let go of our fears. Correct?"

H.S. "Yes, my son of course. The more you can surrender your doubt, your anxieties and fear into Gods hands and let go and let God in other words, the more that you will allow the divine inherent wisdom to seep in through your subconscious mind and into your conscious mind to enable your greater access to your own intuitive direction for each of you with your lists at hand. Helping each of you complete and realise that which you wish to manifest in your own lives. Whether this is simply to express your own creativity, whether in the arts or business or whether to help others in whatever way is your own calling to do so my son."

S.H. "So, when we trust in love, that love occupies also within us that space into which worry and fear creeps into. Mostly, our own minds through the gaps created by our doubts. To either imprison or disempower us from manifesting our full potential. Instead, into the gaps once held by doubt the divine loving creative intelligence to which we have swift access through our intuitive mind springs eternal to guide us on the currents of love that our higher wisdom is carried on."

H.S. "Yes, my son you can only access that wisdom whilst your mind and emotions are peaceful and present in the now moment, to reach the fullest potential of which you are able to manifest in any lifetime in which you find yourselves.

Choose love, not fear always. When you are disturbed by fears - remember you have the choice to choose again – choose love - let love always be your guide my son."

S.H. "Many of us get trapped by 'victimhood' – by thinking of ourselves as a victim, to some event or another. For example, when a relationship ends. Particularly a relationship that we did not wish to end. We prolong the hurt and pain in our own mind, by thinking of ourselves as a victim to the choice of another, due to the fact they wished to end the relationship. It is normal to have a period of grieving. Yet, I think, the sooner we can let go of the grief and move on the better.

I have learnt we can either choose to be a victim of such circumstance, or choose not to be. What has helped me upon realisation of such, is not to revisit the pain body but to take myself out of it each time I return, by choosing not to feel like a victim of circumstance. Instead, to remind myself that I am divine love and that I do not need another's love to either be happy or survive. For we are all love. We are all loved. We are all the source of that love."

H.S. "Indeed, my son. Well said, you are that. All are that. You are all that and yet, so much more too, as this discourse on awakening is revealing to you all here!"

SHARING THE HUMAN EXPERIENCE

S.H. "It is natural though to seek other human contact and a connection with others, especially with others of like mind to ourselves. It nourishes us, in a way we all need. A social interconnection, to share a social discourse on one topic or another. It is a need, nearly all of us hold close to the core of our being."

H.S. "Yes my son, this is natural. Not just within humanity, but many other life forms too. It is about feeling a sense of oneness and belonging to and being with others. It is a sharing of the experience of being human, of being alive. This is again where a sense of belonging and a sense of community comes into question. It is about being part of a community of sharing with others. It is a need which comes in part from feeling a sense of purpose in life. A feeling that you count to others. That you are appreciated and loved. We acknowledge how difficult it is in the human experience not to feel a sense of separation and disconnect from others and all that is around you. In the human experience the sense of separation is strong – especially if you over identify with your body as being the true extent of your true complete being – which it is not – so, as we are endeavouring to teach and pass on to you now in this spiritual dialogue.

It is we know, difficult not to think of yourself as just the body, when that is the limitation of your experience here on Earth, as a human being. This is where your capacity for expanding your awareness, your consciousness comes into the equation.

Notice and remember the interconnection with and to all life forms. Connect as much as possible through your ability towards love, compassion and empathy and your heartfelt knowing, by opening to the currents of love within you all."

S.H. "Is there a way more of us can share this heartfelt connection of our human experience than we do already?"

H.S. "Yes my son. By looking after others more than you do already. By spending more time thinking of and serving others with greater need than your own. By helping those who are sick, whether in mind or body, to heal themselves. To helping your environment and all other life forms to heal, survive and thrive. By eliminating all from your lives that has a detrimental effect on any life form on your planet.

If you could all see your planet and all life forms it supports as the totality of your body and look after it as if it were – as it is in truth – it would be cared for so much more deeply, and once more start to thrive as a loving entity in itself. At the present time, Earth does not feel loved by humanity as a whole, but neglected by your activities.

This will change in the fullness of time as we have already told you. See the Earth as an extension of yourself and care for her accordingly."

S.H. "I was thinking earlier in my daily meditation about the disconnect between people, even though we are ever more connected with our digital devices. Yet, the paradox is that its effect is one of greater disconnection, rather than a greater connection. This is I feel because the connection is non-personal. There is no direct connection with the other person when it is through devices, unless there is a very deep heart connection between two individuals which is very rare in my opinion."

H.S. "Yes, my son, there is a disconnection from the spirit with the other. You are not connecting energetically with the other. You are connecting with the inanimate device, rather than the energy animated by love with another individual. This connection feeds your soul in a way that a man-made object cannot do so. There is a sharing with another individual which does not occur with an inanimate object. When you converse, and share with another you are connecting at deep level with another on a spiritual level whether you are aware of this or not. You see in them a deeper part of your own self, which feeds your own self and sense of belonging to a community of oneness greater than yourself. This does not occur when you shut yourself off for long periods from human connection with others by getting caught up with your devices. This is the cause of some cases of depression where there is a lack of social discourse, because individuals have chosen an electronic device over human company or contact or a connection with nature by being out in nature and connecting with that which surrounds you in that moment my son. You cut yourself off at your own peril."

S.H. "How could we all share our human experience so that it improves not only our lives individually, but also those of humanity please?"

H.S. "My son, welcome back to our discourse here. It has only been twenty-four hours, but you have been on your own private journey these last few hours have you not? The journey of which we speak is crossing a threshold of uncertainty, in connection of the transition from life to death. The experience of the unknown whether for oneself or for another individual. When the other person is someone very close to us it is natural to feel a strong sense of 'dis-ease'. We are afraid of many things perhaps. Including how the passing of someone such as a close relative will affect our own lives and inner stability. We are concerned for their loss as well as our own, yet we do not realise at such times of distress is that throughout this process of pre-grief, where we cannot be sure whether or not it is the time for one soul to pass from this life to the next, we doubt our own capacity to cope with their loss from the perspective of our own lives. The other person assuming a strong bonding in the relationship, often leads to a form of dependence of one form or another. It is because of this bond with the other, that makes us fear when that bond could be broken by the person no longer being on the Earth plane as a companion or close relative, and all the love and support which accompanies such a relationship.

Of course, as our teachings here have continuously stated there is no separation whether you are in the body, or not occupying human form. The spirit of the departed one is still close on an energetic spiritual level. In fact, when there is a strong bond of love through spirit, you will discover through in part your own sensitivity to such energy, that their presence will feel even more permanent and closer than when they are on the Earth plane, even though you cannot communicate in the way you once would have."

S.H. "Thank you for these reassuring words. The person in question, is feeling better. I felt a bit selfish, as I thought if they died that my writing would have been suspended, as a result my own ensuing grief for their passing. Although my main concern was about the person in question of course.

How does this answer my previous question though about how many of us would improve our sharing experience for ourselves and others though?"

H.S. "By improving the quality of their time we have left in life with those persons we most care about to enhance each other's lives with love and support however we can. By communicating with love and compassion, by attending to their needs as best is possible.

Wherever you can share, help, communicate with others. Always, if you can with a smile rather than a heavy heart. Even with a heavy heart, this can still be done and will help the one as a result who is suffering still my son.

The answer holds no complication or surprise, it is remarkably simple – love!"

S.H. "Thank you. So, you could say then simply that the more we can share, communicate and spend time in the company of others, especially those with whom we share a bond, the more we can improve the quality of our lives. I also suspect this will be of course to the benefit of our health, mental, physical and emotional. The opposite of this would point to why so many people are lonely and how and why they suffer so much through their loneliness."

H.S. "Yes, my son indeed, to feel loved, another needs human company, even though that is what you are – it is the paradox of the human condition and why so many people find it difficult to feel self-love for themselves!"

MOVING FORWARDS IN TIME

S.H. "My books purpose is to help other people raise their own level of consciousness about their true spiritual identity. That we are all one in spirit – to encourage sharing and living in unity through peace and understanding. There is if you focus on positivity, a great positive movement about this if people can keep their focus away from the main-stream media, which reports mainly on negative news. I want to deliver good news, uplifting news, as much as possible, through the information that is shared here to hopefully benefit others."

H.S. "Yes my son. You are right and we support you in your efforts, quite literally. We would recommend however, a note of caution – do not think that you can change the minds of others whose minds are closed, 'for they do not have your ear'. They will try to undermine your work, if it is a threat to their own livelihood, or deeply held personal beliefs. Do not allow yourself to sink to the level of argument for the sake of changing that which refuses to give your voice a chance to be heard.

Speak your words and leave your writing and sentiment with others and allow that. If your truth resonates with them, they will incorporate such beliefs if they resonate according to themselves. Be gentle and patient in your approach. Allow the fruit of your labour to grow slow and deep in the hearts and minds of those who are drawn to your message here. For life is a pathless land to truth – for each finds their own path, to their own truth, although truth is the one you all share in your being.

Life is a journey through many selves, through many experiences of trial and error, suffering, hurt and loss. Success comes from these things. It is through your failures that success springs eternal, for in the mind's eye of success, are a thousand failures, unseen by others only self – the one-self is not unaware, that is why the 'one true self' is guarding, helping, supporting each one of you on your own path, along your own journey, to reclaim that which was lost but will be found again. That is your own inner truth and resonance with that.

Your own inner resonance with truth speaks to you in many ways, as it does for all others too.

All the problems and issues faced by your world are of humanity's own making. By this we mean humanity has created its own world, through its actions and priorities according to what humanity believes to be true.

What humanity has believed to be true for most of its past, is that to live well and be successful in life, means to take, rather than to give. To receive, rather than to pass on, whether this be wisdom, or material possessions. What humanity often do not realise, is that in the giving comes the receiving. For life rewards those the most who give rather than take. Your true nature is to give if you allow such. Your heart expressed is your heart giving love. To receive love is because you are love as we have told you many times. Love goes to love and hate goes to like. Like is drawn to like, even at the energetic frequency of being.

You will draw unto you, that which you give out. If you give out fear – you will draw fear to you because of the nature and resonance of fear, it is drawn to itself.

Love is drawn to love. Keep your words, actions and motivations always on love and love will build around you and your loves. When you spread this out to your greater communities of being, you can see how this love can spread in your world to make your world more harmonious for all the creation it supports. Whether it be on land, sea or in the air. Your future rests on the generation which follows your own. They will spread this love across your shores, from place to place, from land to land until the return of the winged ones of old who once occupied your lands and you live in total peace and harmony with nature. They are the sacred tribes of old who spread across your lands, across your continents. The indigenous tribes who lived in harmony, not just with themselves, but all that they came into contact with. They are slowly returning now, one by one, to reinvest this sacred energy of love and wisdom and to share it with others to raise the consciousness of humanity to the next level that is required now to restore the healing into the hearts and minds of many men and women. To cast out fear for love to return. Your digital media will resist this for only so long until the forces of love outweigh the forces of fear sufficiently for love to take the upper hand in all your places of power and influence across your lands, around your planet. The wise ones who once walked your Earth before this time, to return and take their rightful place as leaders towards your planets healing path anew."

S.H. "So, it is a bit like a cleansing right now. A purging of old fearful ways of being which are being cleared out from people and places to make way for the new. An energy, a frequency of consciousness, higher than before. Anchored, by new wise and old souls who resonate more with this new higher frequency of being, who are returning to clear up the mess left behind by others. In many cases a selfish lot of people, not that aware – who have caused a lot of damage to the planet, the environment and a lot of nature and wildlife it holds or once held."

H.S. "Yes my son, you could put it that way. But it is a bit harsh on those people to whom you refer. For example, they to a certain extent were victims of their own upbringing and the conditioning and attitude which surrounds them at any given point, as those here now are also influenced in a similar way. The many benefits now being the freedom of this new informational sharing and the ability for information to reach people and not be controlled by governments and others if it is not to their own liking. In some places this is possible but is becoming increasingly difficult as in the vast majority of places this information is readily available and therefore more difficult to suppress without violent unrest ensuing because of any such attempt to suppress such information. Your books are their own example of this. You are sharing this information to help enlighten others to help enable a better future for all by teaching others about love and unity in their true nature and being and to express this in each moment to the best of their ability for the benefit of all."

S.H. "One of my favourite sayings is – 'Complexity is my confusion. Simplicity my enlightenment.'

I feel that a good teacher is a person who can make the most complicated things sound simple, or can explain such, so that they are easy to understand. I try to do this to the best of my ability, especially in my writing. Much understanding, I think, is missed by people because they have the perception that 'it', whatever it is, will be too difficult for them. So, they do not even try to understand It!"

H.S. "Yes, my son, the mind opens or shuts to your understanding. Your heart also, the true seat to your wisdom. Your knowing within. Listen always to that. Your true way of knowing. Listen to the inner teacher. The 'in – tuition'. This is the voice of your wisdom inherent within you all. These messages do not come on the frequency of words or sentences but on the filaments of light frequency far beyond such, for they are instantly installed or downloaded into your being and without the lumbersome need of translation from one language to another. For they come to you on the frequency and in the language of which all share in their hearts. These feelings do not need to be translated for they are known to you immediately in your receptive state of being. When you are calm, when you are at peace within yourselves, cultivate and encourage this state of being at harmony, in tune with the moment to allow these feelings of divine inspiration and knowing settle upon your consciousness like the morning dew. Lightly it falls. Softly it speaks to you. To each moment when you listen. When you ask for such guidance within yourselves, whatever it may be about for the help in the moment.

This is the greatest knowing within you all. You each have your own resident teacher within yourselves. You do not need books to teach you. You do not need spiritual teachers or gurus to guide you. You each have your own such wisdom resident, living within your own soul and hearts. This is truly who you are. How you were born to be. Before you even came into this, your now present life in which you find yourself you existed in a state of bliss and union with God. All of this wisdom was available to you then as it is now. Simply step out of your own way. Let go and let the guide within guide you in each moment. Be present and let God be present in you as much as you are able to allow the divine wisdom flow through and sustain you in your true way of being and interacting in your world and with others."

S.H. "Indeed. Our minds keep getting in our way often holding us prisoner to our own repetitive thoughts and emotions which block our inner channels to our own inherent peace, love and wisdom. It can be so annoying to say the least.

That is why this whole 'zeitgeist' movement towards meditation, mindfulness, yoga, plant based living, exercise – I find it all so positive and encouraging. It all seems to be tapping in to something bigger, a 'global unity of consciousness'. Raising the thought and consciousness of all towards greater sharing and unity and much greater consideration of our planet, environment and all living things held within its arms."

H.S. "Yes, my son. This is the movement now. No - projectory. The direction in which humanity is moving in the most positive of ways. Do not look to your media for confirmation of this. There you will only find fear and false hope. Look instead to the social media and sharing of your young people. They are the ones who truly care, for they are the ones who will inherit your Earth. They are the ones who care. They see with different eyes to your eyes. To the eyes of your generation. Today is a new generation, on a new earth. They do not care in the same way for the trinkets of materialism. For the false gifts made at the social expense of others to please themselves. The generations of today are the generations of your tomorrow. They have come with a mission. That mission is change. To change your planet. To change your attitudes. To change your priorities. To change all that needs to change in the minds and hearts of humanity to raise global consciousness sufficiently and beyond to instil, install and integrate these new attitudes, beliefs and ideas also into their own children's minds, to carry this change further still, in time to be received by the creator as the creator planned for humanity to slowly emerge from its chrysalis of being into the butterfly that humanity was always intended to become. To fill the world with a beauty of being, never seen before on your Earth. To engage with peace, as peace was always intended to be on planet Earth."

OUT OF DARKNESS INTO LIGHT

S.H. "It sounds then as if humanity is truly on the move now then. Moving literally from one chapter of humanity's being into another chapter. This new chapter sounds like massive changes in the way humanity lives is going to change for the better towards a new brighter Earth and way of living. Hopefully not with too many birthing pains?"

H.S. "My son, this shift, this process of change has been a long time in the making. Each of your generations has played a part in this change one way or another. Your generation were the last and yet the first warriors of light. You have come to help humanity make this transition from a very dense, fixed place within the minds and hearts of men where materialism had taken a strong hold. You and others like you, have simply come to help them release the hold that, that mind-set had on the minds and hearts of men. You, like others have come to soften their hearts to allow themselves to be more receptive to these spiritual messages riding the currents of love straight into their hearts. So long shut down to their true nature and resonance of being. Love cannot penetrate a closed heart or a closed mind. You and your words here have but one purpose. To open them up!"

S.H. "Good. I hope our words achieve this wherever possible. Wherever our words find a crack or crevice and the light and this information from realms of light can enter to facilitate this change however possible. There are so many others out there sharing this same or similar message. Teaching many others to open their hearts and minds to the greater spirit and love which birthed and sustains us all. Love is the way. Awakening to love is the way forwards towards this change in all areas of our being, our living, our sharing. In our homes, in our communities. In our countries and in our world."

H.S. "Your world my son is moving through time. Yet the moment is forever present if you allow it. Life's purpose is for life to discover itself and celebrate in its own discovery in the material realms of matter. In the spiritual realm, there is no sense of the spiritual. It is as difficult there to comprehend as it is for you here. They are different worlds and yet they are one. There is a crossover between the two. The bridge which connects them both is the love you each hold in your hearts. The more love you allow to enter your hearts, the more that love can bridge the two worlds, you see. The more souls from spirit will cross into your world to facilitate these changes of which we speak. The more warriors of light will be called across these bridges to face the challenges to come in your future my son."

S.H. "Yes, we really are going through a big shift right now. I can feel it. It feels as if the shift is happening on so many levels: personally, socially and globally. A lot of people I suspect are feeling quite insecure in themselves for many reasons. Worried about their future. Even the planets future with the various changes and challenges it faces for creation and its environments. I do hope that we can get things sorted out to save us all from destroying ourselves and so much else on the planet. It would be a great tragedy should we fail!"

H.S. "My son. Do not fear. Now is the time to relinquish fear once and for all. Your purpose here and now is to spread your message far and wide as much as possible along with those others who have a similar calling. Each has their own mission here to accomplish. It is no coincidence that your skills are being put to use at this time and that all the platforms and technology now exist to support this in a way it was not supported previously, in your recent past even. Utilise your skills and opportunities to share this information – much of which you already know, and release it into the world like wild seeds on the wind to find a home to grow in the hearts and the fertile minds who can support and express these teachings for the greater good of humanity.

Your prime purpose for sharing these words and the riches they bring to your soul for expressing your creativity in this way is reward enough, any other form is secondary. Keep your focus on this purpose my son and release any other expectations which will not satisfy your soul as you have already begun to discover my son. Measure your success not on what you see appear before you but what you feel in your heart about this process, for that is your true reward for your efforts."

S.H. "Yes, I understand that. As you know I have found myself getting a bit obsessed with how my previous book in this series is doing. My tendency is to become a bit obsessive about things that I get involved in. Sometimes this is good because it helps me to be proficient, but I don't want to tip across the line and become too obsessive so that whatever it is becomes an unhealthy situation. "

H.S. "Yes, that is your tendency indeed. However, if you simply keep your mind focused on your intention rather than your achievement you will be fine. Focus on your heartfelt desire to share information to help others rather than that which will help you yourself. The former, as previously stated, will be where your greatest personal reward will be felt."

S.H. "How will humanity know when it has crossed the threshold into a new era of light?"

H.S. "My son, your world is on the precipice of this moment. It is a shift in personal values of the population of your planet. It is a shift from fear to trust on a massive scale. A shift from a negative standpoint or view to a positive attitude of being. A trust in the benevolence of being one community. A community based on unity, sharing and support for each other in your families and in your communities spread all around your Earth. This will be a time when an awareness of the spiritual presence of God will be known in the hearts of all beings. It is through this awakening to truth within, that this shift will ultimately occur. This awakening will come on the currents of love which are now entering your eco-sphere at an intensity never beamed before into and on to your planet. This is being felt by all creation not just humanity. This vibration of love is what is increasing the consciousness of all. It is only now that humanity, having evolved to the level that it already has, can accommodate this last push and acceleration of consciousness, that it can be integrated into your being sufficiently safely to allow an orderly exchange from one state of being, to another operating at this higher frequency of love, light and informational exchange at this highest level."

REPLENISHING THE SYSTEM

S.H. "My wife and I are both particular about staying as healthy as possible through our diet and by exercising. We eat a mainly plant based diet, meditate and exercise a lot. I have not always been this way inclined, although I have meditated regularly for over thirty years. Like most people, I have had stressful times and I also had a demanding work career as a police officer. My coping method quite often, was my practice of meditation, which has enabled me to develop my own skills to help stay calmer than I would otherwise when I get either worried or stressed about something. It has I believe helped me to expand my consciousness and it has helped me to realise that I am a witness to my thoughts, rather than my thoughts or emotions that I experience within my being. It has taught me over time how to witness my thoughts and emotions with a greater awareness and clarity on a day to day basis. It has also shown me more clearly the power of our thoughts and emotions that we can all feel day to day. This is both for good or bad. The awareness required to develop these skills is something which we as a species need to incorporate as much as possible into our lives to make life better for all of society. The zeitgeist is I feel moving in this direction. Do you agree?"

H.S. "Yes, my son. It is. Although all are at different stages of their own inner growth and personal development. As we have said many times, you are all connected at the deepest level of your being. When one person learns, and grows at the deepest level – it affects the whole not just of your race but that of the whole of creation.

God experiences also through your experience. There is nothing that God does not 'know'. You are God experiencing life in the human form. ALL OF YOU ARE THAT. It is God – call this force, power, intelligence, by whatever name you wish. The name is meaningless in the flow of time. It is the essence of such, of conscious awareness and inherent in all, dancing in love which is the substance of that which we speak. There are many labels used now, past and in the future for that which you all truly are. Remember one thing children of light – the love which holds you now so tightly, will hold you forever. For all time. You cannot leave yourself. You all belong to each other. You all are a part of the 'other' in the divine ocean of loving oneness shared by all.

Through your eyes this consciousness flows. Share it with each other at the deepest level. When you look deep in to the eyes of a fellow human, you will see divinity staring back at you. The same 'one' which sees the other you behold with your own eyes. Open your hearts as you do at the same time, and your hearts will connect also in unconditional love for what you both share in divine brotherhood of man, of woman, of being human."

S.H. "So, these human inclinations for this deeper connection to our spiritual side is drawing so many of us, consciously or not, towards activities like meditation, yoga, mindfulness, healthier food, lifestyles and similar activities?"

H.S. "Yes, my son they are. For their reasons also, people looking for any ways they can to cope with your lifestyles often in urban settlements, where peace is often more difficult to connect with and mental pollution' caused by such. You are right in your suspicion my son, that when you live in large densely populated areas you can feel the thought structure of others. Thought and emotions create a climate on the 'etheric' level of being. It is something sensitive people can feel more than others. But it is manifest by such turbulence of mental and emotional energy.

We will give you an extreme example of such and how it is possible for such to linger and last in the place of their origin. In places where extermination camps were created during your more recent world wars, the depth of the emotion and mental anguish are etched on the ether of such places and domains. If you visit such places your consciousness will sense the suffering which took place there. This is an extreme example, but it demonstrates the power of thought, to affect the environment in which they occurred, and how this energy can last a long time. This energy can be cleared over time by the opposing forces of love, when sufficient numbers of people emitting this frequency, do so over time in the same immediate locality. It is like healing a wound to the etheric 'ether' of place.

Your world as such does not suffer with this affect generally speaking, only in a few tiny pockets where such tragic occurrences have taken place in your more recent past. Human beings are a powerful force for good not surprisingly.

Humanity though in their naivety have caused such temporary damage to your environment can and will make reparation for and to such damage. This will occur as this higher consciousness envelopes your world brought in part by a shift in the harmonic resonance of divine energy flooding your Earth now and in recent decades. It is also entering your world through the hearts, minds and intelligence of your younger generations who have evolved sufficiently in time gone by to shift your planet to its next stage of growth and healing, to allow the changes about which we are speaking here, to change through their implementation those things on your planet which need to be swept away. You are all now the agents of change. So, use your skills and your knowledge and your health to instil and trigger these changes. Still latent in many, but waiting to flower like the rose to the sun. Shine your own individual light in your paths of choice, through your careers, your chosen paths to explore in this life. Share your knowledge and information as freely as possible with others to help make this change so sorely needed, as quickly and smoothly as possible.

Your world awaits with open arms for the change it so warmly anticipates to come in this new dawn of enlightened souls now dwelling on planet Earth."

THE WOMB OF GOD

S.H. "As I walked down to the hotel where I write these books, I thought of the hidden meaning, to me at least, of a famous movie character from 'Star Wars', called 'Obi-Wan Kenobi'.

I saw the – 'OH-BE-ONE-CAN-I-BE, hidden within this famous yet fictitious character's name. In the film his character played a spiritual teacher. He taught about the power of the force, and the connection we all have on a spiritual level with one another. Also, about the fight of good against evil. The essence of the message in this book is the same – remember to be the one – that we can be. That we are all ONE, all of us connected to all that is, through our divinity."

H.S. "Yes my son, you are that indeed. The message was hidden to some, not to all. Sometimes, what is obvious on the surface remains invisible to many. So, it is with the essence of life itself you see. All around you each, is evidence of this connection to all things. All around you, is evidence of the connection to life and all that sustains life. Through the cycle of the seasons you see the hidden pattern of life and rebirth. Why should this apply to nature and not to yourselves?

You see people die, and you see in the next second a child born. You see in one moment an elephant born and then one die. Life is permanently recreating itself in its own vision of itself. The cycle of birth and death is shared by all. Within the circle there is no end,

Awakening to Love

there is no break in a circle, it is continuous. Around and around it goes. Within its circle all life is contained.

The Earth is a circle. The sun is a circle. If you could see the universe from the outside. It itself, is a circle held by love. There is no outside of the circle for outside is love also and this in truth is the etheric world. The world of spirit to which all matter returns. It exists within your universe and yet outside of it, in another realm of being. Yes, your universe is a circle too, surrounded and permeated by love. Like a child, your universe is held in the body of God, like a child is held in the womb of the mother. The universe is that child of God, at the same time permeated by God, as the body of the mother permeates the child held within her body and supported by love. So, yes, your universe is infinite. There is no end to its domain. But it does not continue outwards to infinity. It continues outwards into the infinite which is God and is held by God within and without."

S.H. "When I was a boy I remember saying to my Grandad, "do you know Grandad, that the universe goes on for ever and ever?"

He replied to me, "don't think about things like that or you will go crazy".

I've always remembered that. But I was not afraid that I would go crazy. I just found it hard to imagine something like our universe going on and on into infinity."

H.S. "My son your grandfather was himself curtailed by his own fears and this is what he was reflecting to you in this instance. However, such is your nature for enquiry into the realms of matter and being, that you had your own vision and desire to find the answer to your own nature of being. This was your own soul's call in searching for itself. You had a knowing deep within you of the source of your being to which you had temporarily fallen asleep. Your life has been a journey back to this source of your being, as much for your own sanity, as the need for love which you so often feel within yourself. It is this yearning for love, that had driven you forward in all your endeavours to seek the answers that you have been seeking. Your soul would cry out to you, to find your way home to the deepest aspect of your being.

So, it is within most people my son. The desire to fill the void of emptiness that so many feel within their lives. The unfillable void, as we would call it here in the realms of non-matter. The spiritual realms, where your souls return for nourishment and solace not just on death, but in your sleep also. This is a main factor why sleep is important and not just to rest the body, but to nourish the soul also my son. This is unknown to many, because it is not what you are taught in your schools or universities. But in time even this will change, as mankind awakens to their true spiritual nature – the source of their being. You are helping to show the way here with these words, helping to spark a light within the deep recesses of minds to which these truths have been closed for so long. So, awaken now, once again we say to you, to that which you all are – oh-be-one-can-you-be!"

TRUST IN THE PROCESS

S.H. "How can we be the success that we want to be in life and what is the best route to this success?"

H.S. "My son, what are your goals?

What is your aim?

Is this financial success, or is it instead to find joy, peace and contentment in your own life and helping to elevate that, in the lives of others?

Many people find financial success but not joy, peace and happiness. Which bears the greatest riches my son?

What use is great wealth if you do not also possess health, joy and happiness. Money then has little value, does it not my son?

Do not measure your success in life, by your bank balance alone, my son. If you have sufficient funds to live the lifestyle you wish for and are content with, then you are already wealthy and successful.

This is not a matter of simply being grateful for what you already possess, but what you can give to others.

In this process of writing for you personally, you wish your endeavours to be successful and reach as many people as possible, in part for the reader's possible spiritual enrichment but also for your own. For your ego's enrichment and for your own personal enrichment my son. What we are trying to remind you here with these words is to keep your eye on the bigger picture. Measure your success on what in yourself this process brings to you, in your own self-worth and sense of personal accomplishment, through using your own skills and writing ability to bring forth this information, so that those other persons who choose to do so, can do so freely and make up their own minds about the personal validity of the message presented here to them. Do not pre-empt the message my son. You are the purveyor of the message but not the recipient in the true sense. That person is the reader. The effect of such on them is beyond your control and will forever be a mystery unto you. Allow that, respect that is a part of this process. The lesson contained within this process, is to have trust in each stage and allow this journey for you to unfold as it is my son.

Focus on your endeavours being a success by all means, but allow serendipity to be the outcome of your wishes through the divine workings of universal law and karma. Many wheels operate within many wheels of being, in a complex chain of events, one cannot occur before another. Allow the process to unfold in permanent trust, as best as you can allow such my son."

S.H. "So, in other words, you are saying be grateful for what you already have. For what you have already achieved, and if you are already content, be grateful for that. Focus on that and allow for greater achievement, if that is meant to be a part of one's fate or destiny?"

H.S. "Yes my son. Exactly. Be grateful for what already is. Many blessings have already been bestowed my son. This does not mean stop working at your endeavours. But, simply remember each day to hold gratitude in your heart for the many gifts and good fortune already bestowed within your own life. Continue to focus on spreading your light, love and wisdom where you can and where others approach you for such. You realise your own worth and inherent abilities and you are learning to share what you can to those who have an ear for your words. Remember not all will listen. Not all will be drawn to this information. For some it will not resonate. This is the order of things. Each are drawn to that which resonates within their own selves, their own truth, their own beliefs. Many roads, as they say, lead to God. Many different paths to further spiritual enlightenment. Each must choose their own path. There are many paths which ultimately lead to the same place - AT ONE WITH GOD!"

S.H. "In my own case my desire for success is also hampered by a lack of patience. I think I struggle, due to a lack of patience. I want things now, often. Like many do. What can you say about patience and to those who have the same difficulty remaining patient?"

H.S. "My son what is patience firstly?

Is it not making an allowance for time to bring to you, that which you desire most, whatever it might be i.e. fame, fortune, love, romance?

Whatever it might be for the individual.

What we would say, is the key to making room for such to enter your life, is to make room for the very thing you wish for most. We will take the most common one for most i.e. money.

If you wish for more money there are various obvious avenues to procure more money lawful or unlawful. Using your skills and gifts in a job, being one of the most obvious.

However, what is unknown to many, is wanting will only lead to wanting.

Knowing, will lead to that which you 'know' being manifest. When you trust, and believe that which you desire to come to you, will come, then you have unlocked the secret of manifestation. Trusting and totally believing in your own power to manifest that which you desire, is the key. Therefore, if your wish is for your books which you write are to be very successful, know and trust in the process that this will be the resulting outcome. Do not doubt, for doubt is what blocks the flow of universal energy to bring about the desired outcome. For when there is doubt, the energy flow pauses. When there is trust, the energy continues to flow under the direction of the power of your thought and intentions. When your thoughts centre around not believing in the process, whatever it might be about, then the universe listens, it hears doubt – so doubt is the result. When it hears trust, then that is what happens, the universe trust's and the energy flows once again in the direction towards your desired outcomes. This is how the powers of your individual manifestation works. The universe listens to your commands. When you doubt such, the universe responds because of your doubt and the process of manifestation is halted temporarily, until you stop doubting. Continue trusting and the universe then continues moving forwards towards realising your intentions and wishes. This is your gift and power that each possess as regards the power to manifest. TRUST IN THE PROCESS, my son. Much love to you."

S.H. "In the previous question we touched on something which I feel I do now fully understand. I can understand how doubt can stand in the way of our being able to manifest something in our lives. I can understand how trust can help. I think what I need more guidance on and to help me understand more fully how doubt can prevent manifestation of something, be it temporary. How can this be so?"

H.S. "My son, the doubting process throws a spanner in the works of your own manifestation power, because the universe acts on what thought you hold 'now' in each moment. If it is doubt about manifesting something in particular, in this instance as it is topical and relevant, let us use your book as the example. If you are doubting that your book might, or will not sell well, then the echo's or vibration or ripples of that thought or idea i.e. that your book 'might not' or 'will not' is the 'bait' if you like that you cast out into the ocean of being and creation.

You cast out 'might not' or 'will not', instead of, my book – 'will be a success'. Do you see my son?

Your wish is the command.

'My book will sell well. It will be a success. It will uplift, help, and teach many, about various spiritual truths to help them in their lives'. Hold this thought in trust, without doubt in each moment. Do not allow doubt. When you keep the attachment to this outcome however, you make it less difficult for doubt to enter the process. However, if you keep watching how your book is selling and performing on certain rankings, your anxiety about it failing or sliding down the ranking will only lead to greater doubt. If you detach and focus elsewhere on other matters, then doubt as regards the process of your book doing well, will diminish, and trusting it is, and will do well, will return. The universe then hears your trust, and it will perform better as more people will be drawn to it by their own divine guidance. That is one of the miracles of the universe and how it moves in mysterious ways, as few people are aware of or understand, that this is one of the processes in which the universe and the power of manifestation operates my son.

This does not mean that you cannot or should not do anything to help your book do well, or whatever else you are trying to manifest. But it is about the nature of your thoughts about the process. Trust rather than doubt, being key here my son.

Focus also, is good and important. Again, as long as it is positive focus and not negative focus, which would just be another term for self-doubt. For when you doubt, you are denying the power of and belief in the greater self which you are all part of. This is indeed the very reason you all hold this AWESOME power, if you believe. This, because you are all part of this greater self as we have been telling you. That is why it is possible to manifest this way because of that great connection. Each is connected to the greater whole. Each part hears a part of the other. It is how and why the 'zeitgeist' is!

Seize and allow this knowledge through the greater good and use it always with good intent and may love be your guiding force always and purpose behind such."

S.H. "Thank you. I understand better now, how doubt can stand in the way of self-manifestation and how trust in each moment can encourage, support and help deliver one's intention and focus on a task or desired outcome whatever it might be."

H.S. "Exactly my son. You must make room and allow your desired outcome to be manifest with patience. Time is the other part of the equation. All things take time, so you must also be patient and allow the outcome to be made manifest in a way unknown to you. The outcome may be made true by means other than you expected. Patience is the gift that delivers itself unto you. In the way, you trust now that this book will eventually be manifested. Trust also in the same relaxed, calm manner that your book will do well and reach many people where it is most needed at the time my son."

SURRENDER TO DIVINE POWER

S.H. "It is easy to compare ourselves to others about our ability and our achievements. Always there will be greater and lesser in terms of such. It is easy when we compare, to become disheartened or feel tempted to give up in some way. To lose trust or faith in our potential and abilities. Maybe it is particularly at such times that we need to draw most strongly on our trust and guidance in divine power the most?"

H.S. "Yes my son. Surrender to divine power. That power is within you all. It hears your cry. Pray, ask to be shown, to be helped. If you harness the power of your passion and your gift to others you cannot fail. It is in the nature of the love of God to help those who serve God for the benefit of others. For God wishes only to serve and help others, for all are of God. Kindness is key. Service is the joy of the creator to bring joy to others held within the realm of God. It is that power which sustains all you see, as we have told you many times, my son. Do not be disheartened. Often the darkest moment is just before the dawn. Let go and let God do your work. All of it. Let God draw your audience unto that which you have birthed into the world for the benefit of others. Others will be drawn to the resonance of such gifts. Within themselves they will know if your message resonates with themselves. If not, so the gift will be provided by another who resonates more. Each is drawn to a different frequency. Yet all are drawn to words of truth in whatever form they take. Your message is yours, and theirs is theirs, each one similar and yet different. The essence of the individual message bearing the imprint of the personality of the author. That is what makes each gift to others unique. It bears the signature of the provider with the essence of its message. To that is the other drawn. Not the words. But the essence, the vibration of those words contained on the page before them."

S.H. "Yes, the uniqueness of the individual is what makes each person and each work of art, or whatever they produce in life a reflection of themselves. Their thoughts and beliefs. Their very essence and energy comes through in their work whatever it might be attracting, those especially who resonate with that also. Thank you for this timely reminder once again with my own efforts to help manifest my own expressions of my being to help others. I have realised being new to it that the world of books is a busy and competitive world. Many have been involved in such far longer than myself. Sometimes you can feel that you are an imposter and have no right to enter the world that they inhabit. However, when I do think along those lines, I try to trust in my own self and my own gifts."

H.S. "Indeed, you have much to offer and you are helped to deliver the information you yourself once sought so readily for the sustenance of your own soul to help you at your own times of difficulty. Did you not my son?"

S.H. "Yes I did. In the way that I was helped at such times, I wish to now do so where I can, in part to help express my own creative skills to make this information available to help others. There is a greater need and appetite, even compared to when I was younger and was avidly searching for my own answers.

I want to try to distil the message to as simple a form as possible, so that even the youngest and most challenged person can understand the messages delivered here in essence to help wake them up to their real self and their own power to make a better life and a better world for all. That is my primary intention with this."

H.S. "Yes my son, we understand that, and that is why you are being helped in this way in this process to help manifest the information you seek in a format easily digested by others, to show them the way ahead in their lives to a more fruitful future and greater understanding of these spiritual truths of their being. Life need not be a mystery. Life is meant for living. Life is meant to be a joyous uplifting experience for all. It is the mind, the fears and doubts that it can hold, which most often blocks the passage to these truths. Truths which are always available to the open hearts which welcome them into their being. Remembering always the need and desire to be open to change, to allow room for them to take root in the minds once closed. An open mind and an open heart is all that we ask. An open mind and an open heart can change the world. The more of these, the greater the changes you will see in the world for the better my son. For change to manifest, love must manifest itself where it has not shone its light for so long, my son. Into the smallest crevice light can shine and love can take root and a mighty change can result, which can change your world overnight. The greater the desire for change the greater change will manifest."

S.H. "What is the key to surrendering to divine power?"

H.S. "Good question my son. The key is within you. The key is held by all. It is simply letting go to the divine love and guidance within each of you in each moment. Being in tune. Being in touch with the present, in the 'now' moment. The power of now is that – is powerful – because it is your point, your place of connection to that divine guidance and power. It is through the surrender of your thought and emotions and your capability of such, to surrender and let go, that your capacity to the moment will be made known to you.

It is you getting out of the way. The little you. The small 'I', to make way for the big 'I'. The true 'I', which you are all connected to and are a part of. The universal intelligence. The creator of your being. That intelligence embalmed in love always which holds all in its embrace, my son."

S.H. "So, the theory of surrender is simple. The process being more difficult often for many. But I suppose it is practice. Practicing being aware enough to step out of the way of our thoughts and emotions to create a peace and stillness within, to allow this divine guidance to flow unhindered so that it can be heard and acted upon as necessary, by each person as best they can."

H.S. "Yes, my son. That is so."

S.H. "That is why I have found meditating, quiet and solitude so important and beneficial to me personally to help me to acquire these skills and guidance, as I have so often needed it to guide me through my own fears, doubts and difficulties."

H.S. "These have been your tools of recovery and they are such for many but not all. However, it is always peace, howsoever it is found, that is the remedy at times of crisis. Peace is the way. Peace is the answer. Peace. Choose peace always and the way will open up before you."

THE GATEWAY OF DIVINE UNION

S.H. "Loneliness is a major problem for many people in the world now, as is stress. I see a connection between stress and loneliness. Could you comment please?"

H.S. "My son, indeed there is a strong link between the two. Stress is when the body, mind and spirit are not at peace and out of alignment. Loneliness is when a person feels a sense of isolation from others. But also, when they feel an isolation from their own spiritual sense of self. At such times, there is no sense of joy within the individual on a long-term basis. Short term, yes, they can experience joy through one means or another. But here we are talking about a deep sense of joy which comes from knowing that the individual is connected to the divine spiritual essence, of all that is – which is what they, and all are. If you are not in attunement with this essence of self, you are in turn cut off from that essence in a feeling and sharing sense. You are not cut off from it in truth. Only in a sense of belief or lack of faith and trust that you are that. That of which we speak is what connects you all. If you see a disconnect in that or with that – loneliness will be the result as well as a feeling of stress, in the sense that you will feel vulnerable and alone, like an island adrift on an empty ocean.

So, how do you come to that place of greater self-realisation in self about your greater nature?

Simon Herfet

The answer – that you must go within to that small space of stillness within your heart. Allow within you, love to flow and allow all that blocks that flow to be released through self-love and forgiveness. Into your heart will flow the love and wisdom which guided your ancient ones to the wisdom which guides you still back to that place where self-knowledge and wisdom resides within you.

Stress is a choice, be it an unconscious one. Loneliness is a choice, be it an unconscious one. If you are elderly and live alone and are confined there by infirmity, this is different. But, if you feel in your heart and mind loneliness, this is through choice. For your loneliness is caused by your thought and beliefs held about self and others. Your emotions of pain, doubt, fear and distrust of others creates a barrier between you and them. These emotions likewise, cause much of the stress of which you speak. The individual person, the ego, the character of the person, that which is false, that which is the illusion of self creates the barrier. It is not the loving wisdom held deep which sets you apart. Pass through the gateway – the open door of your consciousness to the greater aspect of your divine being where love holds firm. Embrace and enter that space within yourself. Set free the imposters of which we speak which hold you prisoner in your pain and deluded sense of isolation. For the divine embrace of benevolence and love which hold all as close as your breath holds close to you. Set yourself free and learn to embrace others and self with an open heart. Let service to others be your goal and you will set yourself free from yourself. Free from the mind which holds you down. Free from the loneliness which makes you feel unloved and alone.

Yes, your modern world is stressful enough. But the world has always been a stressful place in which to be and exist. Always, have there been challenges and difficulties and stress is a part of life in the physical domain, if you allow it to be so. Do not allow stress to be a part of your experience. As much as possible banish those things which cause you stress in your life. You will find that there are many that you can change or let go of. Do this wherever you can. Where you cannot, try to change your attitude about those.

Where there is loneliness or isolation in your life, seek to help and love others and self as much as possible. And know through your spiritual connection with all around, you are as much a part of that which you see and feel and hear, as is all else that exists. For you are the source from which your love springs. You are the source of the intelligence you sense and know. Your heart is the gateway to the union and connection with oneness that you all seek."

S.H. "So, once again, the more that we can 'awaken to love', which is our true nature, the more we can embrace this knowing in each moment of our life – the more present in the now we can be. The more mindfulness we can embrace. The awareness we reflect not just within ourselves, but to others too. The more consciousness we can project out into the world. The more enlightenment humanity can share. The more we can raise the spiritual consciousness on this planet. The more we can address the problems which threaten the wellbeing of our inner and outer environment."

H.S. "Yes, my son. Well said. This is so. This is true. The answer is not complicated. The path to that is not complicated. The journey along the path of life is what humanity finds difficult. That is until they have they have been able to attain the knowledge to overcome such difficulty. Ultimately, until humanity can embrace the wisdom to make the necessary changes within and without to restore peace so that your world can be as the divine intended. This is the journey of life experiencing life – for that is what you all are: life experiencing life in the physical realm. That is your joint challenge to find your way home to your true self."

S.H. "Part of the skill of living too, is living in joy. Living in happiness and spreading such to others as much as possible, presumably?"

H.S. "My son you are not responsible for the happiness of another. That is of their own choosing. Only another can choose to be happy, if they choose that. Only another can feel joy, if they choose that. Your responsibility to yourself, is to choose that yourself, if you so wish in any given moment. It is true to say, the more of life that you can bring into the present moment embracing joy and happiness, the more likely others are to be feeling such also. So be that, live that. The best way to reflect that, is to shower your love and radiance into the world. Be a beacon of light and service to others. Let your words embrace and uplift others, so that they in turn can do that for themselves while here on planet Earth."

THE SYNCHRONICITY OF NOW

S.H. "One of the biggest benefits that I have found through my own regular spiritual practice, including a lot of meditation, is that it has enabled me to be more present in the moment, than I used to be in the past. I used to live in my head much of the time. When I was about twenty years old, I developed mental health problems (in part I now believe, due to long term use of antibiotics for acne, in addition to an anxious nature of character) and I became quite ill. My previous day-dream world became a nightmare landscape from which I could not escape. For about two years of that period of my life, I have very little recollection of what occurred. Despite this fact, I was still able to function and perform the role of a police officer, despite my illness, which I chose to keep to myself as best I could. Many years later my diagnosis was anxiety and obsessive compulsive disorder, or OCD. This is recognised as being one of the most debilitating illnesses that there is. I certainly would not recommend it!

However, for me as difficult as it was, in another way it was a gift too. I knew even then, that medication would not be my panacea. I knew that I had to find my own way through it. So, meditation played a key part in my recovery, as well as a variety of other factors including largely, the love that I have received from many other sources. This includes love from many people close to me in the past and the present time.

I am sharing this information because I would feel as if I was being dishonest not to do so, and I do feel also that my own illness has been a major factor in my own spiritual journey, which has in part led to me being able to access the information supplied in this book series.

When you suffer any form of mental impairment, as anyone who has suffered from such will know themselves, that it is even more difficult to stay in the present moment than it is for someone who is not mentally ill.

Over time, as mentioned, the mist of confusion, fear and my doubt lifted sufficiently for me to live a more normal and stable life. I now recognise that I am not my thoughts or emotions and so I have learnt to be the witness to them as much as possible and not to be attached to them as I once did. I notice any negative feelings and thoughts that arise pass more quickly than they once did. This helps me return to a place of peace within myself more quickly. I am then more able to observe within myself the still small voice of peace and guidance to help me to stay attuned to the truth in the given moment."

H.S. "My son, thank you for sharing this information at this juncture. Your experience as hard as it has been for you, is as you know, one shared by many others. The mind is a very powerful tool. The mind needs to be controlled and know who is the master. No one can control their own thoughts as such. However, thoughts like nebulous clouds of ethereal being are made manifest by your emotions, whether they be based in love or fear. Your thoughts at that time, most difficult for yourself, be it many years ago, were born out of a serial number of fears which you still carried then. Some of these fears were born in lifetimes passed, and some influences from this lifetime troubled you too. It was inevitable that they would arise or come to the surface as they did then, at some point in your lifetime. Your soul knew and was aware that this would be so and would reveal itself to be one of the greatest challenges in your own lifetime, my son.

You knew in your own self that your recovery lay in your own inner strength and not in the support of others, whatever their profession or medical aid's. You knew that this was a dark time for your own soul.

Your spiritual search did not begin at that time but your need to find the path to your own recovery and the truth you so desperately searched for was always available to you, whenever you would listen to your own intuition and could trust in that once your fears passed. Your own spiritual gifts and inclinations in this direction as well as your own strength of spirit carried you through this dark time of which you speak."

S.H. "Indeed it did. My own spiritual journey which really started a few years after this period, helped tremendously too. I started to meditate and slowly I started to heal. I want people to know that I am of course just the same as everyone else with the same vulnerabilities and weaknesses."

H.S. "Yes, my son. Do not fear what others might think about your disclosures. For this my son was your own passage, your own initiation of facing these fears of your own, which needed to be challenged. The only way fears can be dealt with is to bring them to the surface so that they can be faced. This occurred for you on an involuntary level, when it did. You have learnt much from this and are able to share and mention it here. No one can come to the light my son without passing through their own darkness. It is a passage that all must make. It is just a different journey for each person in each lifetime, my son."

S.H. "Anyway, I was not planning to share this information, as I am quite a private person really, and do not share such things with people unless they are close to me. I have shared this here though as previously mentioned, because I feel that it is an important part of my own journey of how I got to where I am now as a person. Really, I wanted to talk about the synchronicity of now. But I suppose that is what this is, a time when I feel at a point within myself when I am ready to share something that was life changing to me, but not to others. That is unless they can relate strongly to my experience."

H.S. "Indeed, my son. Such people will be rewarded and will find these words a comfort to themselves also and will encourage them in their own efforts towards a similar recovery in their own way."

S.H. "Yes, I hope so. When you are present in the present moment magic will happen. That is what I really planned to say at this point. Perhaps I have already done that by including this brief story about some of my own life experience.

Why is it that by being in the present moment, so often magic will happen?"

H.S. "When you are immersed in the present my son your focus is on the now moment. That is the intersection of your own being. It is the precise point where all the universal influences of being converge in divine intelligence for those especially who are receptive to their deepest inner knowing. They are led most often by the still small voice within themselves. That voice is the voice that knows, and is most connected to all the actions and activity of beingness of which you are all a part. In a moment of personal disconnection, you are not so aware of your surroundings and the actions and thoughts or intentions of others. But when you listen to your heart which has a greater awareness of such things, you will be led to those things which you term as 'magical' but are just the universe revealing itself unto you. In each moment, you will be met with what you most need to know in that moment. Especially when there is a great relevance to your personal need in that moment in time."

MOVING TOWARDS PLANETARY UNITY

S.H. "So, by utilising and incorporating these different perspectives on thoughts, belief and eventual knowing, by letting go of fear as much as possible and trusting in love we can move towards a greater unity within ourselves and the world as we come together more in spiritual unity. I pray each day for greater unity and peace in our world. I pray for global unity and that we start to treat our planet and all that lives upon planet Earth with a greater reverence. That is my wish, as I am sure it is for many others too?"

H.S. "As we have already told you my son, this is the time of great change for your world. A time of the greatest change. This time of great change is <u>primarily</u> a time of inner change. A great shift of consciousness for humanity. This shift or change has been occurring for some years now, my son. It is not an overnight change. It is a shift in consciousness so profound and yet it is going unnoticed by many who do not have eyes to see, or ears to listen, or the heart to feel such things. Those with closed minds often come with closed hearts. It is never too late to change. But such people tend not to change often, because their fixed ideas hold themselves prisoner, rather than the other way around. It is the power of the mind and your beliefs which hold the destiny of your lands.

As the consciousness grows like a tide of change, the old rigid belief systems crumble, as they already are in so many ways. The minds and hearts of the young bring with them winds of change. A wind of their consciousness will quickly impregnate all your corners and crevices of those that hold on with their fingertips to the ways of old. Outmoded ways of being and thinking, which never truly served you, but belong to times passed are now as dead as your dinosaurs of old. They exist now only as fossils to future generations, not distanced by much in the way of time and yet distanced by eon's in terms of your belief structures and patterns. As long as humanity has seen itself as separate from each other and the creation that surrounds you, difficulty, fear and the absence love has prevailed in your lives. Now a new radiance shines. A new sun shines forth and down upon you. This is a new vibration of self. This is a cosmic radiance, never shone upon any planet in the history of time. It is a time when heavenly light fuses with physical light to produce beings of light in a physical realm. It is only because the vibration of the physical body you now possess holds the frequency able to contain this new vibration of being. It can accommodate the changes in the physical structures of the DNA of which your body is comprised. A new body – for a new planet of a love vibration to take you all further on the journey into the discovery of self, in a cosmic universe of clarity for all beings, where health and vitality reigns supreme and disease is banished to a time like the fossils you find now on your own sea-shores."

S.H. "It is still hard, even for my own self, being someone who likes to think positively and to be hopeful of change, that such a difference will occur anytime soon. A lot of things still appear very bleak right now. I have even stopped following the media news for this reason. Personally, it is at times to stressful to watch. I hope that

I am not being like the proverbial ostrich, just putting my head in the sand?"

H.S. "No my son. You are not. You are simply refusing to give your energy and attention to the negative news feed, which feeds your consciousness with information which simply causes stress and anxiety in many people who give it their attention.

We are not saying, 'ignore it all'. But to not give it excessive attention, as this will only be detrimental to your health, as it is to many others who do so.

Let yourself relinquish the grip it once had. Keep your focus on positive uplifting messages my son, and spread the news which encourages people to step into their own power. For humanity has long been supressed by dark forces of the disinformation which so often reaches your eyes and ears. This is a form or method to keep you feeling small or insignificant and powerless. Yet, humanity has realised in greater and greater numbers, that you do have a great power for change when you come together to resist and stand up for change to those aspects of life which are wrong, immoral or detrimental to your wellbeing or the planet in general.

It is through your coming together to resist, change and show and encourage your politicians, that you all will not allow such people to occupy positions of power, unless they deliver the changes that humanity now yearns to see made manifest in so many areas of life.

As the consciousness grows quickly now, especially in your young, this swift tide of change will bring many changes which will be evidence of this shift in global awareness for the need of many changes in such places as agriculture, your environment and the general health and wellbeing of your societies at large. Persons of a negative attitude and inclination of being will find it increasingly difficult to function and operate in a society which places wellbeing at the forefront of its priorities in the governing of society.

Trust in these words. Trust in this information. Even though a part of you may still doubt this information. Look around **you, do you not see evidence of such change already? In your** young, even in the older generations, there is a movement towards many changes of that which we speak. The desire for change, will create the changes. Embody the changes you wish to see and it will be so. Share your information and beliefs freely with those open to listening to such. When the tide changes, it cannot be resisted. Allow it to be so my son."

A GLIMPSE INTO THE FUTURE

S.H. "Can you suggest more ways in which we as nations on various continents can all live in greater peace and unity?

As one global community. One way that comes to my mind, is if borders were no longer recognised and as if all land existed as one country and we all spoke one language. Both such features would be the ultimate indicators of living in global unity, surely?"

H.S. "You could say that my son. Yes. But there is still some way to reach this point in your evolution of being as far as humanity is concerned. There are centuries of your culture and those of others to contend with, including language. In time countries will begin to merge in this way. The European Community is a case in point. Your own country (the U.K.) is going through its own difficulties with resistance to such change. However, even here wisdom will prevail. Have no fear that it will not. The more frictionless your borders are in the main the more prosperous and peaceful your countries become. There is resistance to this to prevent the flow of migrants for economic purposes. This is one of the greatest fears of your more prosperous countries and their economies. Your countries do in some respects see themselves as conglomerates in a business sense. As money making machines paying subsistence to your working people.

It is only through a great shift in spiritual consciousness and awareness of your global human population as a whole, that the shift of which we speak will bring the necessary change to facilitate this eventual outcome. You can see from what is outlined here, that great upheaval is the most likely cause of such change, but it does not have to be a pre-condition for such change to occur.

However, human stubbornness and resistance to change is the reason why the former will be the cause of such change eventually manifesting on your planet. The order of things is made manifest by a greater power than a few individuals, my son. There is a new world approaching your shores."

S.H. "What will this new world be like then. Tell me?"

H.S. "My son, this new world will be one which you do not recognise with your limited vision. By this we do not wish to insult your intelligence. The world will operate in all respects from the basis of love. All decisions, from the smallest to the highest level, will be made from the premise of love. What is the best decision for the whole. The whole being not just humanity but all of creation on your planet. For the wellbeing of the planet also. For your environment and every aspect: ocean, land, air, your entire global environment. You will by then be aware of the sacred nature of all creation. You will know how you are connected to 'all that is'. It will be as if it was inconceivable that the creation and manifestation of matter by the divine intelligence could be treated in any other way than with such devotion, love and respect for mother Earth than how it should have been intended all along.

Yet this recognition and way of being must be accompanied by a level of consciousness not yet prevalent on your Earth. When it is, such changes will be made manifest for all to see and enjoy.

When this change has fully revealed itself, and this will take another thousand of your Earth years to manifest fully, your species will have radically changed. Not just mentally, emotionally through the new consciousness that you as a race will embody. But, every aspect of life on Earth will have changed, so that your lifestyles now, will seem prehistoric to those that inherit your current Earthly systems of being.

Your current human thought systems are based primarily on a resonance and conditioning of fearful outcome. When your perspective and conditioning is based on love through experience of such, every action is based on the premise of love. Every thought, word and action becomes a reflection of this at all levels of life. This is how and why such great change will occur in your societies. It is also the reason why so much else will evolve beginning at a cellular level in your bodies chemistry, to that of the physical infrastructure of your societies communities. Your technology will also be loved based, rather than profit based. The prime decider will be: is this beneficial to 'all that is'?

Your world will be seen and revered as sacred to all. Your relationship to the animal kingdom will be one of peace, harmony and trust in each other. Fear will belong in another age, as your animal kingdom will become as brothers and sisters unto you all. Have no fear my son, these changes blow strongly in the wind in your 'now' time."

S.H. "This sounds like very radical change to me – be it maybe some way off into the future. I hope it all comes to pass for future generations and I thank you for this information that you share here with me each day that I attune to and write these words. I ask to be used as a pure channel as much as possible to be able to stand to one side in my mind and let these words flow through me."

H.S. "My son, it has been your own souls calling to be used in this way. In part to feel a sense of fulfilment in yourself, but also to help shine a light for others towards a path open to others also, if of their choosing also of course.

There are many paths which lead to the connection with the divine, always inherent within all. It is simply a case to make way within 'self' to allow the essence to flow within self and be led by it as much as possible, through trust and with the intent of loving action always. This in truth is humanity's gift to the world, when humanity lives in accordance with the divine spirit within themselves. It is through the wisdom being in action on your planet that the true healing can occur. This is dependent on the number of your species i.e. 'humanity', who can listen and connect through this new consciousness now coming in and flooding your planet to create this uplift of awareness of 'self' – the true self.

Allow it to flow freely and easily my children of light, it is your birth-right. It is your pathway to your passage back to the heaven on Earth God has long intended for the destiny of your planet, to manifest a body of peace for all creation on the firmament that you call planet Earth. This a radiant beacon of hope to other civilizations far away in your own galaxy who watch on unknown to your own race. Time and space, separates you. But spirit holds you close always my son".

S.H. "Will civilizations on other planets make themselves properly known to us one day? Perhaps, in the near future."

H.S. "My son, your civilization on Earth is a young civilization. In time terms, much like a teenager. Hence your civilizations immaturity to being and the true essence of being. When your race has evolved further and is sufficiently developed in spiritual knowledge throughout society and peace reigns in a permanent fashion, then such other civilizations will make themselves known to you and not before. This is forbidden in the Galactic hierarchy of being."

S.H. "I understand that thank you. Perhaps now we can summarise the message from this book. The second book in the series 'Awakening to Love'.

In the first book, we covered more on the awakening process. That we are not the mind or the body, but that we are consciousness.

All of creation being a part of the ocean of consciousness, which you could call 'God', if you wish to put a label on it.

In this book, I have tried to cover some aspects of how we can awaken even more to the realisation that we are that 'ocean' of consciousness of being. How we can move forward with that self-realisation. How we can surrender more of our fear, by trusting in the divine love and wisdom that we each hold within ourselves, if we can get out of our own way, so to speak.

Finally, to help encourage society on embracing this self-realisation, to take the next most natural step through cause and effect to live as a global community with and through this joint knowledge. To come together as one human community irrespective of any visual difference, to live together in a greater loving, peaceful unity."

H.S. "Yes, my son. Well said. That is your wish and the divine plan for humanity, and it will be so!"

Thank you for reading this book and I do hope it has inspired and informed you. If so, then I would be most pleased if you could take a moment and leave a review on Amazon to help others find this information to help inspire and uplift them on their journey of discovery about their own spiritual nature. Simon Herfet.

Printed in Great Britain
by Amazon